T0196430

Why My Blood Is Enough

JUSTON NAIL

WESTBOW°
PRESS
A DIVISION OF THOMAS NELSON
& ZONDERVAN

Copyright © 2014 Juston Nail.

All rights reserved. No part of this book may be used or reproduced by
any means, graphic, electronic, or mechanical, including photocopying,
recording, taping or by any information storage retrieval system
without the written permission of the publisher except in the case
of brief quotations embodied in critical articles and reviews.

Scripture taken from the King James Version of the Bible.
Scripture quotations are from The Holy Bible, English Standard Version®
(ESV®), copyright © 2001 by Crossway, a publishing ministry of
Good News Publishers. Used by permission. All rights reserved.

Scripture taken from the *Amplified Bible*, copyright © 1954, 1958, 1962,
1964, 1965, 1987 by The Lockman Foundation. Used by permission.

*Scripture taken from the Holy Bible, NEW INTERNATIONAL VERSION®.
Copyright © 1973, 1978, 1984 by Biblica, Inc. All rights reserved worldwide.
Used by permission. NEW INTERNATIONAL VERSION® and NIV® are
registered trademarks of Biblica, Inc. Use of either trademark for the offering
of goods or services requires the prior written consent of Biblica US, Inc.*

WestBow Press books may be ordered through booksellers or by contacting:

*WestBow Press
A Division of Thomas Nelson & Zondervan
1663 Liberty Drive
Bloomington, IN 47403
www.westbowpress.com
1 (866) 928-1240*

*Because of the dynamic nature of the Internet, any web addresses or
links contained in this book may have changed since publication and
may no longer be valid. The views expressed in this work are solely those
of the author and do not necessarily reflect the views of the publisher,
and the publisher hereby disclaims any responsibility for them.*

*Any people depicted in stock imagery provided by Thinkstock are models,
and such images are being used for illustrative purposes only.
Certain stock imagery © Thinkstock.*

*ISBN: 978-1-4908-5865-4 (sc)
ISBN: 978-1-4908-5866-1 (hc)
ISBN: 978-1-4908-5864-7 (e)*

Library of Congress Control Number: 2014919540

Printed in the United States of America.

WestBow Press rev. date: 02/13/2015

Contents

Acknowledgments

I received revelations from God about writing this book while I was cutting grass. I did not start studying for it until six months later. During that time God kept urging me to start working. I constantly thought about it. I told Lela, my wife, that God kept drawing me to the project. She said, "Well then, you need to start it." So I did that Friday night. I could feel the Spirit of the Lord guiding me through it. That following Sunday the book was confirmed by God and by someone who did not even know about it. As it was coming to a close, the Lord told me to contact WestBow, the publishing company, about any promotional discount. I did, and it turned out that they were running a sale that would end the next day, which fell on a Friday. I lost my debit card, so I had to take the money out of my bank account the next day to load it on a prepaid debit card. Friday came, and I was able to make the down payment to hold the deal. God saved me a good deal of money. I was required to make two month's worth of payments. The first month I thought I was not going to be able to make the payment because I was a little short on money. Being a daddy of four children and a husband, it is hard to make it on a small salary, especially since my wife is a homemaker. Many of you probably know where I am coming from. At that moment God provided me with additional work to cover the cost down to nearly the dollar. Praise God! Then the next payment came along the next month. It was due on a Monday. The Friday before I did not know what I was going to do, but I trusted in the Lord. I prayed to him, "Lord, I do not want to be late on the payment. I believe in my heart that you will provide the money to pay for it." That evening someone told me they had the money they owed me from a side job I had done. When they paid me, it was more than I thought it was, but it was just enough for the last payment. The whole time God was along for the ride. When I got discouraged, he provided the income to make it happen, and he provided the spiritual reviving either through a prophetic word or through some other means. He would remind me that he is faithful to his Word that he will never leave us or forsake us.

I would like to thank my wife for being so understanding and supportive, my aunt for always being there for me, my co-workers for their support, my church family, and my friends in Atlanta, Georgia. But most importantly I would like to thank my Lord and Savior, Jesus Christ. Not only did he take all the wrong that I have ever done to the cross, but he also called me to be his servant. No matter where this book goes and how many lives it touches, it is all because of his love made it possible.

Introduction

God has shown me many things that affect the doctrine at some churches. It is the same Bible we all read, so why are there so many different interpretations? Many people don't follow the Holy Spirit and take the time to study for themselves. They rely on their tradition and the creed of their assembly.

Too many do not understand how easy it is to obtain salvation. It is so easy that the unlearned and even a child can do it. Too many times we do not think that salvation alone is purchased by his blood. We rely on baptism to complete the confession unto salvation. But we do not know what baptism is for. Why do we do it, and why does it not secure our salvation?

We rely on our own *works*, not knowing what works are truly for, what they earn us, and why our works do not earn us salvation.

What's the purpose of the law. Why keeping the law will not save us and why the law is still good now? Too many times men make up their own traditions in churches and their own law.

Finally what was the purpose of so many different sacrifices in the Old Testament? Why don't we need to make sacrifices any longer? Why was Christ sacrificed? Why is faith in Christ's sacrifice enough for salvation? My prayer is that there will be souls won over to Christ and barriers broken down between denominations by the end at this book and that we will all know why his blood is enough!

Baptism

What Is Baptism?

According to the Greek translation of the *Strong's Exhaustive Concordance of the Bible*, baptism is a ceremonial wash.

Baptism is a ceremony performed by all denominations. Most will agree that it is not the key to salvation, but few people understand its purpose. The first baptism was Noah's flood. The flood was God's way of passing judgment on all of mankind for their sins. It cleansed the world from all unrighteousness by water, and only eight righteous people were saved (Genesis 6:17; 1 Peter 3:20), then the baptism of Moses (1 Corinthians 10:2). The baptism of Moses was when the children of Israel were leaving their past life of bondage and were beginning a new life as followers of their savior. The next baptism was not performed until John the Baptist comes along. John the Baptist was the forerunner for Christ. He was to evangelize the nation of Israel for the coming of Christ (Malachi 4:5–6; Luke 1:17).

John's baptism was a baptism of repentance, but it was incomplete (Mark 1:4; Luke 3:3; Acts 19:4). It was just to prepare Israel for a new way. They were under the law, and their forgiveness of sin was done through faith in Jesus Christ. They just were not aware of it. Many today rely on baptism as their savior. If baptism did save, then John the Baptist would have been the Messiah, and there would have been no need for Jesus. However, many did believe that Jesus was John the Baptist (Matthew 16:14).

What Is Baptism's Purpose?

Romans 6:3–4 (ESV) says, "Do you not know that all of us who have been baptized into Christ Jesus were baptized into his death? We were buried therefore with him by baptism into death, in order that, just as Christ was raised from the dead by the glory of the father, we too might walk in newness of life."

When we are baptized in the name of the Father, Son, and Holy Spirit and when we announce the Godhead during our baptism ceremony, we are showing others who are watching (or even if we are alone) that we are partaking in his death, burial, and resurrection. We are showing that the water of judgment has passed over us and that we have died to the world (Amos 5:24). We are now new creatures, no longer sinners (Romans 8:1; 2 Corinthians 5:17). Without true conviction baptism is pointless! When I was eighteen years old, I was deer hunting in Pickens County, Alabama. I was reading my Bible. Suddenly I experienced an overwhelming flood of emotions, and instantly I knew that I was a sinner (Romans 3:23). The Holy Spirit convicted me of all my sin and all the wrong I had done (John 16:8). I was surrounded by his presence and his love, and it engulfed me! He showed me that without his forgiveness I was destined for hell! At that moment I believed in my heart and confessed with my mouth that he was the Lord of my life!

With this new Spirit in my life I finally realized how rude, mean, and plain ugly I was to my mother. I called her immediately to tell her I was sorry for all the hurtful things I had said to her. We both cried together on the phone! That is the power of forgiveness! I went nearly ten years before I was baptized, and I backslid many times throughout the years. That is why discipleship is so important. Christ actually commanded us to teach all nations (Matthew 28:19, 20). If you are a pastor of a church and you are not teaching the Word in depth to your sheep, they will never grow in Christ! You must feed them not just a Sunday morning repentance message but a Wednesday evening in-depth study so that they can grow from milk to meat (1 Corinthians 3:1-3; Hebrews 5:13, 14).

Christians, if you are saved and not following God's Word, you will never be happy! You will always fail! God does not want that. He wants to give you hope and a future (Jeremiah 29:11). And whatever you do will prosper (Psalm 1:3). But you must learn who he is and what he expects from his children.

I finally grabbed a hold of God as the Rock of my life (Psalm 40:2; Matthew 7:24). He called me to repent for the sins in my life not because I was lost and going to hell but because sin breaks fellowship with him. Once I cleaned up those issues, he then called me to preach! Praise God! At that time I finally got baptized.

Baptism Represents Faith in Christ's Resurrection.

Colossians 2:12 (AMP) says, "[Thus you were circumcised when] you were buried with Him in [your] baptism, in which you were also raised with Him [to a new life] through [your] faith in the working of God [as displayed] when he raised him up from the dead."

I like how the Amplified version of the Bible brings out (Colossians 2:12) a little better. It says, "When you were buried with him in your baptism, in which you were also raised with him to a new life through your faith." We are buried with him during our baptism as a symbol to the world that we our dying to our old ways. When we come out of the water, we are raised with him in a new life through faith. Our faith in our Creator is what gives us eternal life.

Although this is much similar to Romans 6:3–4, there is a significant difference. We see that it is God that raised him up from the dead, but our faith in God through Jesus Christ is what is required of us. Faith is the key word. If faith was not involved in baptism, then it was not legitimate. Faith must be present.

Water Baptism Is a Commandment!

Even thou water baptism isn't a requirement it is still a command to be done. Mark 16:16 says "He that believeth and is baptized shall be saved; but he that believeth not shall be damned"

Christ gave a commandment for baptizing, but we must also believe (have faith) that he is able to save us and wash us clean of our sins by the power of his resurrection. When the Ethiopian eunuch asked Philip "here is water; what doth hinder me to be baptized?" (Acts 8:36). Philips answer to the eunuch was "if thou believest with all thine heart, thou mayest" (Acts 8:37). Philip made it clear that baptism without faith is useless. Because the baptism ceremony is a work, we know that it will not save us (Ephesians 2:8–9). We are commanded by God to be baptized. If we are Christians, we should not have any shame in being baptized (Romans 1:16). But we should rejoice at it. We are now a new creature, the redemptive work of Christ himself. If you are baptized soon after the new birth, then you will be less likely to fall under peer pressure and turn away from Christ just as the first-century saints. At that moment everyone will know that you are follower of Jesus Christ. Salvation is a free gift that you don't earn, purchase, or deserve. If salvation is received any other way than "believing and confessing in what he did," then we added to his death, and he died in vain (Galatians 2:21).

The Actual Washing Is Done by Jesus, Not by Baptism.

Ephesians 5:26-27 says "That he might sanctify and cleanse it with the washing of water by the word, that he might present it to himself a glorious church, not having spot or wrinkle, or any such thing; but that it should be holy and without blemish."

The washing that cleanses us can only be done by Jesus Christ. This is by the sacrifice and the blood he shed for us (John 1:29; Acts 20:28; 2 Corinthians 5:17). Water is always synonymous with the Holy Spirit (Titus 3:5). Every time you see water in either in the Old Testament and New Testament, you will see the Spirit of God. We are washed by the Word of God by accepting his Son! If you have not accepted his Son, then you have not been washed by the Word, and damnation is upon you (Mark 16:16; John 3:18; 14:6; 2 Thessalonians 2:12).

The Spirit Does the Washing away of Sins, Not the Water Baptism.

Titus 3:5–7 says, "Not by works of righteousness, which we have done, but according to his mercy he saved us, by the washing of regeneration, and renewing of the Holy Ghost; which he shed on us abundantly through Jesus Christ our savior; that being justified by his grace, we should be made heirs according to the hope of eternal life."

Jesus' sacrifice is what gives us a new life. The Holy Spirit is also a synonym for the blood of Jesus. If it was not for his blood, then there would have been no Holy Spirit. By the mercy of God through Jesus Christ, we now have been made "heirs according to the hope of eternal life" Titus 3:7.Our washing and regeneration is done by the Holy Spirit. The Spirit does the convicting and the purging of sins (John 16:8; Titus 3:5). His mercy (his own blood), which was shed on Calvary, was given to us abundantly. Blood was the ultimate sacrifice that was needed to have our sins washed away. It was necessary for the removal of our sins (Hebrews 9:22). This is the only way to obtain salvation!

"For by one spirit are we all baptized into one body, whether we be Jews or Gentiles, whether we be bond or free; and have been all made to drink into the Spirit" (1 Corinthians 12:13).

Paul makes it very clear in his letter to the church of Corinth that it is the Holy Spirit that brings us in unity as one body. The baptism (washing and cleansing) is done by the Spirit, not by water. This makes it obvious that the ceremonial baptism represents that which has happened already on the inside. "If any man be in Christ he is a new creature" (2 Corinthians 5:17). In the first point is this passage he goes onto state that "whether we be Jews or Gentiles." In other words, God does not care whether you are black, white, yellow, brown, or red. All who call on the name of the Lord will be saved (Romans 10:13). And we can do so "whether we be bond or free." Thank God we are all free here in the United States! This can also apply also to the wealthy employer and the underpaid employee. God makes no distinction among the people here on earth based on their finances. He loves us all. As Scripture says, "All to be to drink into one spirit," God came to humanity to save us from our sins. He didn't' make any distinctions between color, gender, or finances. You, too, can be saved. No matter what anyone has told you, Jesus loves you!

Has Anyone Who Was Not Baptized Ever Been Saved?

In short, yes! There are numerous times recorded where people were saved by faith during Jesus' ministry. For instance, "Son be of good cheer; thy sins be forgiven thee"

(Matthew 9:2), "Thy faith hath saved thee; go in peace" (Luke 7:50), "Receive thy sight: thy faith hath saved thee" (Luke 18:42), "neither do I condemn thee: go, and sin no more" (John 8:11), and received the Holy Spirit after his resurrection that was not baptized. Receiving the Holy Spirit has nothing to do with being baptized! Someone once told me that when you are saved, you receive the Spirit but that you are not saved until you are baptized for the remission of sins. The Holy Spirit dwells within you because you are the temple of the living God and God does not dwell within an unclean temple (Acts 17:24; 1 Corinthians 3:16; 2 Corinthians 6:16)! You do not have to wait for baptism to be clean! Jesus makes you clean by the power of his blood! As you continue to read, you will see how people in the New Testament and how born-again believers receive the Holy Spirit before baptism.

The Sinner on the Cross

Luke 23:39–43 (ESV) says,

> One of the criminals who were hanged railed
> at him, saying, "Are you not the Christ? Save
> yourself and us!" But the other rebuked him,

saying, "Do you not fear God, since you are under the same sentence of condemnation? And we indeed justly, for we are receiving the due reward of our deeds; but this man have done nothing wrong." And he said, "Jesus, remember me when you come into your kingdom." And he said to him, "Truly, I say to you, today you will be with me in Paradise."

Just at the time of death on Calvary, the two sinners next to Christ were sure their lives were coming to an end. One criminal refused to accept Christ, and his fate was sealed for him! Do not be the one that is to hardheaded to realize you need help! But one sinner humbled himself and admitted that he needed someone who was perfect and able to save him from hell. As the saying goes, "There are no atheists in the foxholes." At the point of death many have received salvation. Many have died and went to hell. If you are not right with Christ, do not wait until the last minute to repent. As you can see, there was not any water present. Some have said that he may have been baptized before he repented. That is incorrect! If he was baptized before he repented, then his baptism would be insufficient. If he lost his salvation after he was baptized, then he would have needed to have been baptized again (if baptism is necessary for salvation). This means that more is required than indicated here, "If we confess our sins, he is faithful and just to forgive us our sins, and to cleanse us from all unrighteousness" (1 John 1:9). Then it would be necessary to be baptized again. Nevertheless, baptism was not needed for this man to enter into heaven. This sinner was high on the cross. There was nothing but him, Christ, and repentance. If you are relying on baptism to save you, you are never going to make it to heaven. You must rely on the cross!

The New Birth on the Day of Pentecost

Many were already saved before the day of Pentecost but there were one hundred and twenty people in the upper room on the day of Pentecost. Those one hundred and twenty received the Holy Spirit without being water baptized. Acts 2:1–4 says,

> And when the day of the Pentecost has fully come, they were all of one accord in one place. And suddenly there came a sound

from heaven as of a rushing mighty wind, and it filled the entire house where they were sitting. And there appeared unto them cloven tongues like as of fire, and it sat upon each of them. And they were all filled with the Holy Ghost, and began to speak with other tongues, as the Spirit gave them utterance.

Some say that this is when they were all baptized with water because it was prophesied by Jesus Christ (Acts 1:5). This baptism had nothing to do with *water baptism*. This was the baptism of the Holy Spirit. Many were saved on this day, and many were already saved because they believed in the resurrection of Jesus Christ (John 20:27–29). As they were filled with the power, the presence, and the glory of God, they spoke in other tongues. There was no water baptism, no special deeds, no special works. It was just believing in the name of the Son of God and receiving the fullness of his Spirit! Peter did tell the crowd in Acts 2:38 "be baptized every one of you in the name of Jesus Christ for the remission of sins, and ye shall receive the gift of the Holy Ghost." Baptism is a synonym with receiving salvation. It is much like being baptized in the name of the Father, Son, and the Holy Spirit (Matthew 28:19) or in the name of Jesus Christ (Acts 2:38). It truly makes no difference which of the two passages you are baptized into and it makes no difference if you are baptized or not to be saved. You must "believe in your heart and confess with your mouth" to be saved. As you read you will see how salvation is received through confession alone.

Saul's Salvation on the Road to Damascus before He Was Baptized

Acts 9:1–18 (ESV) says,

> "But Saul, still breathing threats and murder against the disciples of the Lord, went to the high priest and asked him for letters to the synagogues at Damascus, so that if he found any belonging to the Way, men or women, he might bring them bound to Jerusalem. Now as he went on his way, he approached Damascus, and suddenly a light from heaven shone around him. And falling to the ground he heard a voice saying to him, "Saul, Saul, why are you persecuting me?" And he said, "Who are you, Lord?" And he said, "I am

Jesus, whom you are persecuting. But rise and enter the city, and you will be told what you are to do." The men who were traveling with him stood speechless, hearing the voice but seeing no one. Saul rose from the ground, and although his eyes were opened, he saw nothing. So they led him by the hand and brought him into Damascus. And for three days he was without sight, and neither ate nor drank.

Now there was a disciple at Damascus named Ananias. The Lord said to him in a vision, "Ananias." And he said, "Here I am, Lord." And the Lord said to him, "Rise and go to the street called Straight, and at the house of Judas look for a man of Tarsus named Saul, for behold, he is praying, **and** he has seen in a vision a man named Ananias come in and lay his hands on him so that he might regain his sight." But Ananias answered, "Lord, I have heard from many about this man, how much evil he has done to your saints at Jerusalem. And here he has authority from the chief priests to bind all who call on your name." But the Lord said to him, "Go, for he is a chosen instrument of mine to carry my name before the Gentiles and kings and the children of Israel. For I will show him how much he must suffer for the sake of my name." So Ananias departed and entered the house. And laying his hands on him he said, "Brother Saul, the Lord Jesus who appeared to you on the road by which you came has sent me so that you may regain your sight and be filled with the Holy Spirit." And immediately something like scales fell from his eyes, and he regained his sight. Then he rose and was baptized."

Paul was on his way to Damascus to slaughter Christians. He was chopping them up, cutting them up, and stabbing them! He was killing Christians with no remorse! This shows us no matter how many sins you have committed or how many people you have killed, "his grace is sufficient for you" (2 Corinthians 12:9), and you can still be forgiven! Not only that, but God can place the highest calling of the universe on your life! He can make you a preacher of the gospel. He can change your lifestyle, your habits, and your personality.

How many of us are like Saul, doing what we please and hurting whomever we please? But God has a plan for your life! All you must do is "seek his righteousness" (Matthew 6:33). Many church leaders want you to believe that your past disqualifies you from being called into the ministry or being able to hold certain offices in the church. If that were the case, then thirteen out of twenty-seven books in the New Testament would not have been written. Saul, the murderous blasphemer, wrote them, but as a born again, redeemed man of God!

Don't believe the lies that the Devil tells you. Perhaps he says that you cannot serve God. If God can use a donkey, he can use anyone he chooses (Numbers 22:28). God answers to himself and himself only. "His thoughts are not our thought's, his ways are not our ways" (Isaiah 55:8). What does not seem to make sense to us does make sense to God! When things do not look possible through your natural eyes, look through your spiritual eyes.

Acts 9:6 in the King James version says, "Lord, what wilt thou have me to do?" Paul's conversion on the road to Damascus is where he chose to follow the Lord. Christ sent him into the field as a preacher of the gospel, but there were things that he needed to do first. He had to have hands laid on him. He was awaiting the man of God named Ananias to come lay hands on him so that he could receive his sight (Acts9:12). I could just imagine all of the shame and all of the regret that he had. He also fasted from "food, water, and sight" for three days to reflect on all the wrong that he had inflicted on God and his people. While he was fasting he was also praying, and God gave him a vision to let Paul know that Ananias was coming to him (Acts 9:11-12). For God to have heard Paul praying he would have had to have been a Christian because God does not hear the sinners pray unless they are asking for forgiveness (Psalm 34:15; 66:18; Proverbs 15:29; Isaiah 1:15; Jeremiah 14:12; John 9:31). Ananias was not eager to visit this murdering man. He even doubted God by questioning his motives (Acts 9: 13).

One drop of his blood is enough to remove all sins and change lives. When Ananias went into Judah's house, he called Saul, "Brother Saul" (Acts 9: 17). They were not brothers in a physical sense, but they were brothers in a *spiritual* sense. He has not yet been baptized with water. He had no special duties, nothing but the calling on the name of the Lord that saved him (Acts 4:12; Romans 10:13). Ananias then laid hands on him and he was filled with the

Holy Spirit (we will discuss being filled with the Holy Spirit shortly.) After he received salvation and was filled with the Holy Spirit, scales then fell from his eyes, and then he was baptized. This incident makes it clear that baptism was not needed for salvation or being filled by the Holy Spirit or receiving healing. But baptism is something that should not be neglected. It is sacred just as Communion and tithing.

The Roman Centurion and His Family's Salvation before They Were Baptized

Many believe that Pentecost only happened once. The outpouring of the Holy Spirit happened all over again shortly later. Acts 10:44–48 says,

> While Peter yet spoke these words, the Holy Ghost fell on all them, which heard the word. And they of the circumcision, which believed, were astonished, as many as came with Peter, because that on the Gentiles also was poured out the gift of the Holy Ghost. For they heard them speak with tongues, and magnify God. Then answered Peter, Can any man forbid water, that these should not

be baptized, which have received the Holy
Ghost as well as we?

The house of Cornelius received the Holy Spirit in the
same manner as the people on the day of Pentecost. Peter
went on to say "and as I began to speak, the Holy Ghost
fell on them, as on us at the beginning. Then remembered
I the word of the Lord, how that he said, John Indeed
baptized with water; but ye shall be baptized with the
Holy Ghost" (Acts 11:15, 16). The Jews could not believe
that they received the Holy Spirit as they did. (Speaking
in tongues is the evidential proof that they had received
the Holy Spirit.) When this outpouring of the Holy Spirit
occurred, water baptism wasn't even thought about until
they were refused the privilege. The Jews did not even want
them to be baptized. This shows that there was a great
racial divide amongst them. Not much has changed. Many
churches are predominantly one color or another. The color
of the congregations should never be the determining factor
when one is choosing a church. It should be the love of
the people and the Word being taught with boldness. God
doesn't care about the color of your skin. He made your
skin anyway.

Cornelius was a Roman centurion. He was a man who feared God (Acts 10:2). But he had not even heard of Jesus Christ. "Jesus is the way the truth and the life, and no man comes to the father but by him" (John 14:6). Although, Cornelius was not saved when he was praying his prayers did come up before God. God could not accept them until he received Jesus Christ into his heart. That is why God sent Cornelius an angel that told him to send for Peter so that he may hear the gospel (Acts 10:3). This makes it clear that God will respond to people who have never heard the gospel but are searching for the Lord of Lords (Hebrews 11:6). People have no excuse for not receiving salvation. Everyone can look at the earth and tell that it has a creator (Romans 1:20). If you can acknowledge that and start seeking him, then you will find him. You must put your faith in Jesus Christ. No other God will save you! Salvation does not come through water baptism. "But ye may know that the Son on man hath power on earth to forgive sins" (Matthew 9:6). Salvation is received by asking Jesus to forgive you of your sins.

What is the Baptism by the Holy Spirit?

This has caused more splits in churches and unbelief in Christians. First we need to understand that there are multiple baptisms.

"Therefore leaving the principles of the doctrine of Christ, let us go on unto perfection; not laying again the foundation of repentance from dead works, and of faith toward God of the doctrine of baptisms and laying on of hands, and of the resurrection of the dead, and of eternal judgment" Hebrews 6:1–2.

What verse 1 is telling us is that we need to leave the elementary doctrine of Christ and go on to maturity. The basic concept of the Bible and Christianity is that Adam and Eve sinned. Therefore, mankind fell. Sickness and disease came into the world. We were separated from God and were destined for hell. God then destroyed sin with a flood and started over with Noah. These are all the principles that Christianity relies on. These are the easiest concepts to understand for nonbelievers. Once we have preached these concepts to people and they have accepted Jesus Christ, then we move on to maturity explaining the different *baptisms.*

What are the different baptisms, and how many are there? There are three baptisms. The first one is the baptism of the Holy Spirit, which washes away your sin. "Not by works of righteousness which we have done, but according to his mercy he saved us, by the washing and regeneration and renewing of the Holy Ghost" Titus 3:5.

You may be thinking that his verse contradicts Ephesians 4:3–8 (ESV), which says,

> Eager to maintain the unity of the spirit in the bond of peace. There is one body and one Spirit just as you were called to the one hope that belongs to your call one Lord, one faith, one baptism, one God and one father of all, who is over all through all and in all. But grace was given to each one of us according to the measure of Christ gift. Therefore it says when he ascended on high he lead a host of captives and he gave gifts to men.

The whole emphasis is *unity*. When there is a unity, there is peace. When you see God move in the early church, they were all of one accord. (They were in unity.) The one Lord refers to Jesus Christ. The one faith is in Jesus Christ.

The one baptism is done by Jesus Christ. Since Christ has paid the price for us, it brought in his one Spirit to baptize us. This baptism brings us into the one body. Then we are baptized with water, which is the ceremony. Then this one Spirit gives us gifts. "Having gifts that differ according to the grace that is given to us, let us use them: if prophecy, in proportion to our faith; if service in our serving; the one who teaches, in his teaching; the one who exhorts, in his exhortation; the one who contributes, in generosity; the one who leads; with zeal; the one who does acts of mercy with cheerfulness" Romans 12:6–8 ESV.

First Corinthians 12:4–11 (ESV) says,

> Now there are varieties of gifts but the same Spirit; and there are varieties of service, but the same Lord; and there are varieties of activities, but it is the same God who empowers them all in everyone. To each is given the manifestation of the spirit for the common good for to one is given through the spirit the utterance of wisdom, and to another the utterance of knowledge according to the same Spirit, to another faith by the same Spirit to another gifts of healing

by the one Spirit, to another the working of miracles, to another prophecy, to another the ability to distinguish between spirits, to another various kinds of tongues, to another the interpretation of tongues. All these are empowered by one and the same spirit who apportions to each one individually as he wills.

Then Ephesians 4:8–13 says,

Wherefore he saith, when he ascended upon high, he led captivity captive and gave gifts unto men. (Now that he ascended, what is it but that he also descended first into the lower parts of the Earth? He that descended is the same also that ascended up far above all things, that he might fill all things.) And he gave some apostles; and some, prophets; and some, evangelist; and some, pastors and teachers; for the perfecting of the saints, for the work of the ministry, for the edification of the body of Christ: till we all come in the unity of faith, and the knowledge of the Son of God unto a perfect man, unto the measure

of the stature of the fullness of Christ.

This passage picks up where the explanation of one Lord, faith, and baptism ends. This is in direct connection with Romans 12 and 1 Corinthians 12. It shows us here that there is one Spirit and one baptism. There are many gifts from the Spirit, and all of these gifts are still available until the fullness of Christ comes. Last time I checked, he has not come to take us home yet. So they are still here and available. This is all about unity. The entire principle of the kingdom and how God operates is enacted through *unity*.

There is one God but three persons to the Godhead, the Father, the Son, and the Holy Spirit—one church body (many people), one head (Jesus), and two people in a marriage (one flesh). There are many gifts by the one Spirit, three baptisms but still done by one spirit that comes as a result from the new birth. The first baptism is the new birth. It washes away the sins of the old man.

"Lie not to one another, seeing that ye have put off the old man with his deeds; and have put on the new man, which is renewed in knowledge after the image of him that created him" (Colossians 3:9–10).

His blood made the purchase for our salvation and ushered in his Holy Spirit to recreate us and move us from a sinful old man to a new creature (2 Corinthians 5:17). This is the new birth that all Christians receive regardless of color, sex, and denomination.

The second baptism, which is to be done after the new birth, is the ceremony that all born-again believers are to do as commanded (Matthew 28:19; Acts 10:48). This represents the old man dying and the new man coming out of the water. This baptism was stressed so much because the new covenant believers were facing persecution from pagan worshippers and the Jewish law keepers (those who had not accepted the grace of God through Jesus Christ). Being baptized in public allowed everyone to know that they had converted and now they had a strong backbone to face persecution. This baptism was the baptism of repentance. It is mentioned many times throughout the book of Acts, and it is also mentioned by John the Baptist and Jesus.

The third baptism is the baptism of the Holy Spirit or the infilling of power. This was prophesied by John the Baptist (Matthew 3:11; Mark 1:8; Luke 3:16; John 1:33). This was not to be done until the day of Pentecost. Jesus spoke to his disciples before he ascended and said "And, being assembled together with them, commanded then that they should not depart from Jerusalem, but wait for the promise of the father, which, saith he, ye have heard of me. For John truly baptized with water but ye shall be baptized with the Holy Ghost not many days hence" (Acts 1:4–5).

The disciples were already born again and received the Holy Spirit, but they were not filled with the Holy Spirit and baptized with power (John 20:22–23). The ones who were not born again received the fullness of the Holy Spirit without baptism or any other special work. The disciples received the fullness of the Holy Spirit without water baptism. When they received the Holy Spirit after Christ resurrected, they already "had believed in their heart and confessed with their mouth." But some would not believe until they saw him and touched him (John 20:24–25). Christ gave him a stern word. He told the disciple Thomas, "You see and believe but those who haven't seen and believe are blessed" (John 20:29).

Those who believe without seeing are blessed. That is us, my friend. We have not seen, but we believe. If they are born again (washed by the Spirit), then why would Christ tell them to wait in Jerusalem until the Holy Spirit would come? See, the Father was sending the fullness of the Holy Spirit to us. This is done to empower the born-again believers! You can receive salvation and be filled with the

Holy Spirit at the same time. It just depends on how much of God do you want in your life!

"But ye shall receive power after that the Holy Ghost is come upon you; and ye shall be witnesses unto me both in Jerusalem and in all Judaea and in Samaria, and unto the utter most part of the earth" (Acts 1:8).

There are several things to mention here. First the Holy Spirit that was to come on them he was giving them power to perform miracles to validate the gospel. The Holy Spirit and power have always been synonymous. Secondly this power is the baptism that Jesus would do, the one that was prophesied by John. To better understand this concept, you could say it like this: "It is the baptism of power." The whole idea of baptism is to submerge the believer. You are submerged with the washing power of the Holy Spirit to cleanse you of your sins. In the ceremony you are submerged in water to represent the new birth, and the baptism of the Holy Spirit submerges you with his power to give you supernatural gifts.

Acts 6:1–8 says,

> And in those days, when the number of
> the disciples was multiplied, there arose
> a murmuring of the Grecians against

the Hebrews, because their widows were neglected in the daily ministration Then the twelve called the multitude of the disciples unto them, and said, It is not reason that we should leave the word of God, and serve tables. Wherefore, brethren, look ye out among you seven men of honest report, full of the Holy Ghost and wisdom, whom we may appoint over this business. But we will give ourselves continually to prayer, and to the ministry of the word. And the saying pleased the whole multitude: and they chose Stephen, a man full of faith and of the Holy Ghost, and Philip, and Prochorus, and Nicanor, and Timon, and Parmenas, and Nicolas a proselyte of Antioch: Whom they set before the apostles: and when they had prayed, they laid their hands on them. And the word of God increased; and the number of the disciples multiplied in Jerusalem greatly; and a great company of the priests was obedient to the faith. And Stephen, full of faith and power, did great wonders and miracles among the people.

The disciples were not able to pray or meditate on the Word and preach enough while they were helping the members of the church. God instructed them to pick seven men (deacons) to help them in their duties to the people. This is where deacons and the help ministry come in. It gives the pastor time to focus on the Word of God, and the shut-ins and the needy of the church are still taken care of. It is selfish to demand too much from our pastors and then complain about the effectiveness of the message if they are spending too much time on our needs. There is a complete balance to God's will. If you are a pastor and cannot handle the needs of the members of your congregation, then appoint leaders, deacons, or help teams. This will keep the people from complaining.

One of the men they picked was named Stephen, and he was full of faith and the Holy Spirit. Luke, the author of the book of Acts, goes on to declare that he was full of faith and power!

See the similarities between *full of the Holy Ghost* and *full of the power*? This power was given to those on the day of Pentecost. This power enabled Stephen to speak boldly against the false teachers (Acts 6:10). He performed many miracles and healings. He possibly raised people from the dead and helped people regenerate limbs. All kinds of things could have happened with a man of God of this magnitude! This power even enabled him to see into heaven (Acts 7:55). The others who were persecuting him could not see what he saw because they were not born again. Nor were they filled with the Holy Spirit. They eventually stoned him for his claim of seeing heaven and preaching with boldness (Acts 7:59). This power enabled him to speak with boldness up to his death.

The key point here that allowed him to be this kind of miracle worker was that he was full of faith and power. It doesn't matter how much of the Holy Spirit (power) God has given out to you. You will never be able to perform a miracle unless you have faith! You must have faith that with God all things are possible (Matthew 19:26; Mark 9:23). If you have been baptized with the baptism of power and have faith that with God all things are possible, then you, too, can see God perform miracles through you.

The Holy Spirit's Baptism of Power: The Infilling of the Holy Spirit at the Day of Pentecost

Christians are able to receive a fullness of the Holy Spirit in our lives. We know that the Holy Spirit is given unto us by measure because Christ had it without measure (John 3:34).

"And when the day of Pentecost was fully come, they were all with one accord in one place. And suddenly there came a sound from heaven as of a rushing mighty wind, and it filled all the house where they were sitting. And there appeared unto them cloven tongues like as of fire, and it sat upon each of them. And they were all filled with the Holy Ghost, and began to speak with other tongues, as the Spirit gave them utterance" (Acts 2:1–4).

When the day of Pentecost happened, it fulfilled the prophecy (Isaiah 28:11; Matthew 3:11; Mark 1:8; Luke 3:16; John 1:33). The disciples had already received the Holy Spirit before the day of Pentecost, but they were not yet filled with him when this mighty wind came. The overfilling of the Holy Spirit caused them to speak a heavenly language (1 Corinthians 13:1). They did not receive this power by having hands laid on them but by believing in him and receiving this free gift and being obedient to his Word. This is the most amazing thing in the Bible to have happened other than Christ dying on the cross and being resurrected.

If you have confessed Jesus with your mouth that he is the Lord of your life, then you have received the Holy

Spirit, and you are saved. What gifts you possess or do not possess have nothing to do with you receiving salvation. Do not rely on what gifts you have. Just put faith in Christ Jesus. He will give you the gifts you need. The infilling of the Holy Spirit is the power Christ told them they would receive before he ascended (Acts 1:8).

The Holy Spirit filling the House of Cornelius with his power

"While Peter yet spake these words, the Holy Ghost fell on all them, which heard the word. And they of the circumcision, which believed, were astonished, as many as came with Peter, because that on the Gentiles also was poured out the gift of the Holy Ghost. For they heard them speak with tongues, and magnify God" (Acts 10:44–46).

Peter preached the gospel to Cornelius's household, and the Holy Ghost fell on them. When this happened, they were filled with the Holy Spirit, and they spoke in tongues. Speaking in tongues magnifies God! It is similar to praise and worship. We are actually told to sing in tongues (1 Corinthians 14:14, 15; Ephesians 5:19; Colossians 3:16). I don't know about you, but I want to magnify God I don't care how I do it! Many people believe that the day of Pentecost was just a one-time deal. But this is a repeat of the day of Pentecost. God's Spirit is still pouring out on believers.

The Infilling Of the Holy Spirit at Ephesus

Acts 19:1–7 says,

> And it came to pass, that, while Apollos was at Corinth, Paul having passed through the upper coasts came to Ephesus: and finding certain disciples, He said unto them, have ye received the Holy Ghost since ye believed? And they said unto him, we have not so much as heard whether there be any Holy Ghost. And he said unto them, unto what then were ye baptized? And they said, Unto John's baptism. Then said Paul, John verily baptized with the baptism of repentance, saying unto the people, that they should believe on him, which should come after him, that is, on Christ Jesus. When they heard this, they were baptized in the name of the Lord Jesus. And when Paul had laid

his hands upon them, the Holy Ghost came on them; and they spoke with tongues, and prophesied. And all the men were about twelve.

Many theologians will tell you that in the old days salvation was received by the laying on of hands. This is not true! Nowhere in the Bible does it say, "Lay hands on them so they will be saved." It says that you should believe in your heart and confess with your mouth and then then you will be saved (Romans 10:9). This baptism gave them gifts (supernatural gifts). Once they were filled, they then spoke in tongues and prophesied. The tongues are an unknown language unless interpreted (1 Corinthians 14:27).

In the Old Testament the Spirit would come on and off of the prophets. Under our new covenant the Spirit remains on us, and we must have his infilling presence to be able to function in this office. The reason why we do not see much prophecy in our churches is because we are not so often filled with his Spirit and the understanding. These gifts empowered the gospel to perfect the saints for the edifying of the body of Christ for the purpose of validating the gospel to non-Christians and to convert them to Christ. Many believe that the apostles were given a power from God and that it could not be transferred to others, but in (Acts 19: 1-7) in Ephesus clearly shows here that it could be.

Many believe that prophecies are no longer happening because the Bible is complete, but that is not true. It is true that no new revelation may be added to the Word of God (Revelation 22:18, 19). The prophecies spoken by the twelve were not recorded, but that does not mean that they are false. It just means that God did not want them recorded. Abel was a prophet, but the Bible does doesn't speak about what he prophesied on (Luke 11:50, 51). There are many other prophecies in the Old and New Testament that are not recorded firsthand.

New Testament prophecies do not predict the judgment of God or the coming of Christ. Yes, the coming of the Messiah is mentioned in the New Testament, and it is no longer needed for mention again. So what are they for? They are for edification, exhortation, and comfort (1 Corinthians 14:3). They give comfort and guidance to individuals. It is another way that God can direct us and teach us. When a prophet of God speaks into your life, you will know that it is from God. It will reveal the secrets of your own heart (1 Corinthians 14:24, 25). There would be no way that the prophet should know about what they have just spoken of to you, and you will know it comes from God! When I have had a prophet speak to me or have seen others spoken to, we normally cry like babies because there is no way that anyone would know what they have said but God!

1 Corinthians 13: 8-10 says, "Charity never faileth: but whether there be prophecies, they shall fail; whether there be tongues, they shall cease; whether there be knowledge, it shall vanish away. For we know in part, and we prophesy in part. But when that which is perfect is come, then that which is in part shall be done away."

Some believe that the phrase "which is perfect" is referring to the Bible being completed. Since the Bible is completed speaking in tongues and prophecies no longer exists or is needed. That is not what it means. It actually refers to Christ coming back for us (the rapture). "For now we see through a glass darkly; but then face to face: now I know in part; but then shall I know even as also I am known" (1 Corinthians 13:12). You see the gifts of tongues and prophecy are here until he comes back (face-to-face) or until we have gone on to be with the Lord. The "for we now see through a darkly glass" means he sees into the spirit only pieces of what God shows him. In other words he only receives "part" of the revelations (prophecies) that God was giving him. Speaking in tongues is not the only gift that the Holy Spirit gives to us. There is also the help ministry (1 Corinthians 12:28). Christ told us that whenever we fed the poor or visited people in prison, we did it to him (Matthew 25:34–40). If what "is perfect has already come," then the gifts of helping have been done away with, and there is no need in helping or feeding those who are in need. But thank God we are called to live and serve Christ with gifts regardless of what they are until he comes back. We are equipped with those supernatural gifts until the "fullness of Christ's return" (Ephesians 4:13). God is still equipping us! Two thousand years means nothing to him! He created time and works outside of time. If the gifts of the Spirit were only for the first-century saints, then the greatest gift, salvation, was only for them. Therefore, none of us would have received freedom from the penalty of sin.

Paul's Infilling of the Holy Spirit

Acts 9:17-18 says, "And Ananias went his way, and entered into the house; and putting his hands on him said, Brother Saul, the Lord, even Jesus, that appeared unto thee in the way as thou camest, hath sent me, that thou mightest receive thy sight, and be filled with the Holy Ghost."

As mentioned earlier, Paul was saved on the road to
Damascus. He wasn't full of the Holy Spirit. But once
Ananias laid hands on him, he received the fullness of
God's Spirit. Although it does not mention him speaking in
tongues at that moment, we do know that he did because
he told the church at Corinth that he spoke in tongues
more than anyone (1 Corinthians 14:18). It empowered
the gospel of Jesus Christ, which he preached. Many signs,
wonders, and miracles followed him. This is a result of
faith and the fullness of the Holy Spirit within him.

The Infilling of the Holy Spirit in Samaria

Acts 8:9–24 says,

> But there was a certain man, called Simon,
> which beforetime in the city used sorcery,
> and bewitched the people of Samaria, giving
> out that himself was some great one: to
> whom they all gave heed, from the least to
> the greatest, saying, This is the great power
> of God. And to him they regard, because
> that of long time he had bewitched them
> with sorceries. But when they believed Philip
> preaching the things concerning the kingdom

of God, and the name of Jesus Christ, they were baptized, both men and women. Then Simon himself believed also: and when he was baptized, he continued with Philip, and wondered, beholding the miracles and signs which were done. Now when the apostles which were at Jerusalem heard that Samaria had received the word of God, they sent unto them Peter and John: who, when they were come down, prayed for them, that they might receive the Holy Ghost: (For as yet he was fallen upon none of them: only they were baptized in the name of the Lord Jesus.) Then laid they their hands on them, and they received the Holy Ghost. And when Simon saw that through laying on of the apostles' hands the Holy Ghost was given, he offered them money, Saying, Give me also this power, that on whomsoever I lay hands, he may receive the Holy Ghost. But Peter said unto him, Thy money perish with thee, because thou hast thought that the gift of God may be purchased with money. Thou hast neither part nor lot in this matter: for thy heart is not right in the sight of God. Repent therefore of this thy wickedness, and pray God, if perhaps the thought of thine heart may be forgiven thee. For I perceive that thou art in the gall of bitterness, and in the bond of iniquity. Then answered Simon, and said, Pray ye to the LORD for me, that none of these things which ye have spoken come upon me.

Simon the sorcerer bewitched the people of Samaria. When you see witchcraft or idolatry, you will always have demonic activity. Satan loves it when people give him recognition. In a place like that, it was full of demonic activity, sin, and probably sickness. We know these things because anytime we give a foothold to Satan, he wreaks havoc in our lives (Ephesians 4:27). Acts 8:6-7 Says, that there were "many mighty miracles and demons were coming out of them." This sorcerer Simon was so amazed at the gospel and the power of the Holy Spirit that he believed and was baptized (Acts 8:12). But they were not filled with the Holy Spirit (Acts 8: 15). It even goes on to say, "For as yet he was fallen upon none of them: only they were baptized in the name of the Lord Jesus" (Acts 8:16).

Then at the laying on of hands they received the Holy Ghost (Acts 8:17). See, there is a separate work here done after salvation, a separate baptism. I once heard that gifts couldn't be given by the laying on of hands, and that same person laughed when he saw in a service the laying on of hands and the people receiving the gifts of the Holy Spirit. Religious people made fun of Christ and his followers then. There is no difference today. People make fun of Christians, and other Christians make fun of each other. It has become ridiculous that we try to tear down one another more than we do Satan. That is exactly how Satan works. That is why Paul told us to put on the armor of God so that we could stand against Satan (Ephesians 6:10–17). The laying on of hands is a sacred practice. Moses laid hands on Joshua. Joshua then received the gift of wisdom (Deuteronomy 34:9). All throughout the four gospels Jesus laid hands on people, and they received healing. The believers in the New Testament early church laid hands on people who received the gifts of the Holy Spirit and healing. Paul told Timothy to "stir up the gift of God that was given to him by the laying of hands" (2 Timothy 1:6). The laying on of hands is an Old Testament and New Testament practice. It is actually a foundational principle for those who have reached spiritual maturity (Hebrews 6:1–2). If we expect to ever reach maturity and grow spiritually, we must accept the whole truth of God's Word.

Simon was amazed at the gifts given to these people by God through the laying on of hands. He wanted this power to make money off of it. On any account he tried to purchase the gift of God with money. Why would God need our money? He has all the money that he needs. You may ask, "Why do we tithe?" Tithing is a sacred ceremonial worship. We pay tithes to God through worship to show him we trust him with our finances. I can just imagine Peter's facial expression when Simon offered him money.

Peter, being the mighty man of God that he was, preached with boldness and acted on obedience. This is what he told Simon:

> But Peter said unto him, Thy money perish with thee, because thou hast thought that the gift of God may be purchased with money. Thou hast neither part nor lot in this matter: for thy heart is not right in the sight of God. Repent therefore of this thy wickedness, and pray God, if perhaps the thought of thine heart may be forgiven thee. For I perceive

that thou art in the Gall of bitterness, and in

the bond of iniquity. (Acts 8:20–23)

One thing is for sure. God's gifts cannot be bought or earned! If you are trying to purchase your way to heaven with deeds, works, titles, or money, you will perish with them all! Salvation is offered to all men, and the callings of God are given to those he chooses to give them to!

When the apostles laid hands on the Samaritans, and they received the Holy Ghost If the experience of receiving the Holy Ghost was merely invisible (it did happen on the inside), then Simon would have not offered money for this power. Simon was already a sorcerer. This Holy Ghost power would have been greater than his own (God's power is greater than anything or anyone, even Satan). This power must have given them the following signs: They spoke in tongues, prophesied, cleansed the lepers, healed the sick, and raised the dead (Matthew 10:8; Mark 16:17, 18). We seek God because we need his salvation, not because we need financial prosperity or some other type of gain. I believe Simon in fear realized when Peter rebuked him that he repented from trying to buy the power of God. He asked him, "Pray ye to the Lord for me, that none of these things which ye have spoken come upon me" (Acts 8:24). Maybe he did repent, and one day soon we can praise God with him for all eternity.

Water Baptism Will Not Save You!

It makes no difference how many times you have been baptized you cannot rely on water to save you! First Peter 3:20–21 says,

> Which sometime were disobedient, when once the longsuffering of God waited in the days of Noah, while the ark was a preparing, wherein few, that is, eight souls were saved by water. The like figure whereunto even baptism doth also now save us (not the putting away of the filth of the flesh, but the answer of a good conscience toward God) by the resurrection of Jesus Christ.

There are several points made in this verse. The first is the flood, which is a synonym for baptism. This is mentioned earlier, but it also stated in Peter. The second point is that baptism does save you but that it isn't the ceremony that actually saves. The baptism that the Spirit does is what saves you. The Holy Spirit does the washing away of sins (1 Corinthians 12:13; Titus 3:5). This is the first baptism of the new believer. The last point is you can only obtain salvation from Jesus Christ (John 14:6).

As mentioned, these three reasons make it very clear that we are not saved by the ceremony but by the washing of the Holy Spirit. Baptism is a ceremony performed on new converts, not a requirement of salvation. We accept this Spirit-baptizing new birth by believing in Jesus Christ!

Didn't Christ Say that You Must Be Born of Water and Spirit?

John 3:3–5 (ESV) says,

> Jesus answered him, "Truly, truly, I say to you, unless one is born again he cannot see the kingdom of God." Nicodemus said to him, "How can a man be born when he is old? Can he enter a second time into his mother's womb and be born?" Jesus answered, "Truly, truly, I say to you, unless one is born of water and the Spirit, he cannot enter the kingdom of God."

Jesus gives us a clear indication about what this water is in John 4.

> Then cometh he to a city of Samaria, which is called Sychar, near to the parcel of ground that Jacob gave to his son Joseph. Now Jacob's well was there. Jesus therefore, being wearied with his journey, sat thus on the well: and it was about the sixth hour. There cometh a woman of Samaria to draw water: Jesus saith unto her, "Give me to drink." (For his disciples were gone away unto the city to buy meat.) Then saith the woman of Samaria unto him, How is it that thou, being a Jew, asketh drink of me, which am a woman of Samaria? For the Jews have no dealings with the Samaritans. Jesus answered and said unto her, If thou newest the gift of God, and who it is that saith to thee, Give me to drink; thou wouldest have asked of him, and he would have given thee living water. The woman saith unto him, Sir, thou hast nothing to draw with, and the well is deep: from whence then hast thou

that living water? Art thou greater than our father Jacob, which gave us the well, and drank thereof himself, and his children, and his cattle? Jesus answered and said unto her, Whosoever drinkest of this water shall thirst again: But whosoever drinketh of the water that I shall give him shall never thirst; but the water that I shall give him shall be in him a well of water springing up into everlasting life. (John 4:5–14)

There was major racial division between the Jews and the Gentiles. Too often here in America we see racial division. When we judge someone, we should do it by looking at the intentions of the person's heart just as God does and not by the color of their skin. Christ didn't come for any particular man but for all mankind. Christ was a gift sent from God (John 3:16). The entire Old Testament was a preparation for the New Testament. The saints of old sowed the seeds for the saints of today to harvest (John 4:34–38). Jesus fulfilled every Old Testament prophecy he quoted.

Jesus knew that he had a divine appointment with a woman in need of spiritual restoration. When the opportunity presented itself, he quoted Old Testament Scripture to her so she would understand the gift he was going to offer her. "Therefore with joy shall ye draw water out of the wells of salvation" (Isaiah 12:3).

He was telling her that he was that gift (John 4: 10). "Whosoever drinkest of the water that I shall give him shall never thirst" (John 4: 14). He is the water that we must drink if we want to be born again. Praise God! This water comes straight from the throne of heaven. "And he shewed me a pure river of water of life, clear as a crystal, proceeding out of the throne of God and of the Lamb" (Revelation 22:1)

This water he is referring to comes from heaven through the wells of salvation and by the Lamb (Jesus). All you must do is ask him for a drink, and you will never thirst again!

"In the last day, that great day of the feast, Jesus stood and cried, saying, if any man thirst, let him come unto me, and drink. He that believeth on me, as the scripture hath said, out of his belly shall flow rivers of living water. But this he of the Spirit, which they that believe on him should receive: for the Holy Ghost was not yet given; because that Jesus was not yet glorified" (John 7:37–39).

Christ tells us that we are to drink of this living water (Isaiah 58:11; Ezekiel 47:1–10; Joel 3:18). His belly shall flow rivers of living waters! The Holy Spirit will live on the inside of us if we drink the water of salvation. The Spirit and new birth was not yet given because Christ has not yet shed his blood for the remissions of sins (Hebrews 9:22). Without accepting Jesus Christ, it is impossible to receive the Holy Spirit. If you do not drink the water Christ has to offer, you will thirst again. That means this life will never be satisfying to you and you will die and go to hell.

In short, the water that Jesus spoke of to Nicodemus was actually himself. It was not a water baptism. Jesus was telling him that salvation comes from him and him alone! If you are thirsty, drink the living water that comes from the throne of heaven (Revelation 22:1–5). This outcast woman had been married five times. She was living in adultery with another man, and she was of a different race. When she tasted the living waters that Christ offered her, it set a fire down in her bones (Jeremiah 20:9). She dropped everything she was doing and left to tell the men in her town about Jesus (John 4:28). That is the type of repentance that God seeks from us! Many people in today's churches would look down on this woman, but Christ did not! When you truly taste salvation, you will not care who is around, who is listening, or what other people think about you! Her repentance satisfied Christ so much that when his disciples returned to him from buying food, they prayed he would eat (John 4:31). Christ told them, "I have food to eat that you do not know of" (John 4:32). This was the reason why Jesus came to us. He wanted to seek repentance from sinners (Matthew 9:13; Mark 2:17; Luke 5:32; John 4:34–38). Does your praise and worship satisfy Jesus to the point where he does not even need to eat? If you drink of this water, you shall not grow faint or become weary. He will increase your strength. You will mount up on wings of eagles and fly(Isaiah 40:29–31).

Why Was Christ Baptized?

There are multiple reasons why Christ was baptized. The first reason was he set the standard for us. We must follow him as a leader and the act of humility just as the foot washing of Peter (John 13:1–17). The second reason is that some churches deny the Trinity, but the Trinity is clearly evident (Mark 1:9–11)—the Father who spoke, the Spirit who descended, and Jesus, who was baptized. Jesus received the Holy Spirit, and God spoke over him. The next reason is that it was to identify Jesus to the people as the sent one by God as the one who was anointed with the Holy Spirit (Isaiah 61:1). He identified who he was by the witness of two or more (Deuteronomy 19:15; Matthew 18:16; John 8:17; 2 Corinthians 13:1).

"And it came to pass in those days that Jesus came from Nazareth of Galilee, and was baptized of John in Jordan. And straightway coming up out of the water, he saw the heavens opened, and the Spirit like a dove descending upon him: And there came a voice from heaven, saying, Thou art my beloved Son, in whom I am well pleased" (Mark 1:9–11).

This shows that there are three distinct persons in the Godhead. There is God the Father. "Thou art my beloved son, in whom I am well pleased." There's the Holy Spirit. "He saw the heavens opened and the spirit like a dove descending upon him." Lastly there's Jesus, who was baptized. When John saw the Spirit descend like a dove on him from heaven, he recognized that Jesus was the Son of God (John 1:33–34). Can you imagine how amazing it must have been to be John the Baptist or some of the people on the bank watching what had just taken place? With all that had happened, there would be no doubt that he was the chosen one sent by God to take away the sins of humanity (John 1:29). The last reason is that it was where he received the power of the Holy Spirit to raise the dead, heal the sick, and set the captives of sin free.

Isaiah 61:1–2 says, "The spirit of the Lord God is upon me; because the lord hath anointed me to preach good tidings unto the meek; he hath sent me to bind up the broken hearted, To proclaim liberty to the captives, and of the opening of the prison to them that are bound, To proclaim the acceptable year of the Lord, and the day of vengeance of our God: to comfort all that mourn."

Luke 4:18–19 (AMP) then says,

> The spirit of the Lord [is] upon Me, because he has anointed Me [the Anointed One, the Messiah] to preach the good news (the gospel) to the poor; He has sent me to announce release to the captives and recovery of sight to the blind, to send forth as delivered those who are oppressed [who are down trodden, bruised, crushed, and broken down by calamity] to proclaim the accepted and acceptable year of the Lord [the day when salvation and the free favors of God profusely abound].

"You know what has happened throughout the province of Judea, beginning in Galilee after the baptism that john preached—how God anointed Jesus of Nazareth with the Holy Spirit and power, and how he went around doing good and healing all who were under the power of the devil, because God was with him" (Acts 10:37–38 NIV)

As John baptized Jesus, he received the Holy Spirit so that he could proclaim the gospel. This validated the gospel. It is also interesting to note that he did not perform any miracles until he received the Holy Spirit. He now had the Holy Ghost's power to do all he was sent to do! This was one of the most important reasons he was baptized.

Preaching the Cross Is More Important than Preaching Baptism!

1 Corinthians 1:17 says, "For Christ sent me not to baptize, but to preach the gospel not with wisdom of words, lest the cross of Christ should be made of none effect."

Baptism is important. It's a commandment given by God (Matthew 28:19). But it does not save (1 Peter 3:20, 21). The way to salvation is through the cross, believing in Jesus Christ as the risen Lord (Romans 10:9). If baptism was the way to salvation, then Paul would have said, "Christ sent me to baptize." Instead he was told to preach the cross because it is a gift to us and we receive it by faith, not by the works (Ephesians 2:8–9).

Why Do We Baptize in the Name of the Father, Son, and Holy Ghost?

All three play a part in salvation. The Father sent his Son (John 3:16). He anointed him with the Holy Spirit to empower his ministry (Acts 10:38). The Son paid the price (Mark 10:45). The Holy Spirit convicts us of our sin (John 16:8). Baptism represents what the Spirit has done for us that it has regenerated us from sin (1 Corinthians 12:13; Titus 3:5) and dead works to serve the living God (Hebrews 9:14). To sum it up, you can say it like this: The Father originated the plan. The Son executed the plan. The Spirit reveals the plan, and we preach the plan. Amen!

Water Is Also a Form of Judgment, and Christ Is Our Savoir.

Water is always a sign of redemption to humanity. Noah's flood is a type of redemption. When God judged humanity sins, he cleaned the earth with water, and Noah and his family were redeemed. The ark saved them. The ark saved them from the wrath of God, and the blood of Jesus is going to save us from the wrath of God in a similar way. The eight people and all the animals had to enter the boat through a doorway. The door is Jesus Christ. The boat is his mercy against his wrath. His wrath is sure to come, but it will pass us by if we are in the boat of salvation (Jesus Christ).

"I am the door; by me if any man enters in he shall be saved" (John 10:9). If we look for this door, we will find it. If we knock on the door, it shall be opened, and we will be saved from our own punishment (Matthew 7:7). He took the punishment of hell, which we rightfully deserve! If you want to be saved from the flood of wrath, then you must get on the boat of salvation through Jesus Christ!

Works

Why Works Do Not Save Us

Your works will never save you "For by the grace are ye saved through faith; and that not of yourselves: it is the gift of God: not of works lest any man should boost" (Ephesians 2:8–9).

Inspired by the Holy Spirit, Paul is telling the church of Ephesus that works do not save us. Works are things done by man. Some are good works, and some are evil works. Many people think their good deeds will outweigh their bad deeds. The truth is that we have accumulated so many bad deeds that it is impossible to pay off debt with our own works of righteousness (Titus 3:5). In our carnal minds we would like to think that our service to people is the doorway to heaven. If we, the good citizens of our country, do all the good things that we could ever imagine and then murder and steal, we will be punished. The judge in court will not let you slide because of a few good deeds. The just judge (Jesus Christ) will not give us a "pass and go" without serving us our punishment unless we have accepted his free gift salvation.

Have you ever bullied, cheated on your spouse, or stole from your employer? God's judgment is so high that he said, "To look at someone with lust is the same as adultery" (Matthew 5:28). Christ also said, "To have anger in your heart is the same as murder" (Matthew 5:21–22). I know that I have been guilty of lusting, but we should refuse to let it take root in our minds! We are not to "be conformed to the ways of the world but be transformed" (Romans 12:2). There have been many times when I have been furious with people. But we must not hold on to our anger. Sometimes we get mad at our spouses, family members, coworkers, friends, and church members. We should strive to work out our problems. Do not let anger turn into unforgiveness. It will destroy you from the inside out!

Paul's letter to Titus makes it clear "that it is not by the works of our own righteousness that we are saved" but by his works (Titus 3:5). If you are relying on your own works to secure your salvation, then you are not going to go very far with God or life for that matter. Your works without Christ involved are compared to filthy rags (Isaiah

64:6). That is how he sees your works without him being involved. The thought of us relying on our own works to save us is arrogant to say the least.

All of the works that we do without love in our lives are nothing (1 Corinthians 13:1–13). Our whole being without him is pointless, and without his works of righteousness for us, we would never be able to stand in his presence (Hebrews 12:29). If we wish to become right with God, we need to accept him as our Master, and then we can become his very own righteousness (2 Corinthians 5:21).

Weren't the Saints of the Old Testament Saved by Works?

No, they were saved by faith in Jesus Christ! Even though Jesus had not died yet for our sins—he wasn't even born for that matter—they still had faith in his resurrection through a promise by God. They just did not have the new birth experience.

Hebrews 11:1–13 says,

> Now faith is the substance of things hoped
> for, the evidence of things not seen. For by
> it the elders gained a good report. Through

faith we understand that the worlds were framed by the word of God, so that things which are seen were not made of things which do appear. By faith Abel offered unto God a more excellent sacrifice than Cain, by which he obtained witness that he was righteous, God testifying of his gifts: and by it he being dead yet speaketh. By faith Enoch was translated that he should not see death; and was not found, because God translated him: for before his translation he had his testimony, that he pleased God. But without faith it is impossible to please him: for he that cometh to God must believe that he is, and that he is a rewarder of them that diligently seek him. By faith Noah, being warned of God of things not seen as yet, moved with fear, prepared an ark to the saving of his house; by the which he condemned the world, and became heir of the righteousness which is by faith. By faith Abraham, when he was called to go out into a place which he should after receive for an inheritance, obeyed; and he went out, not knowing whither he went. By faith he sojourned in the land of promise, as in a strange country, dwelling in tabernacles with Isaac and Jacob, the heirs with him of the same promise: for he looked for a city which hath foundations, whose builder and maker is God. Through faith also Sara herself received strength to conceive seed, and was delivered of a child when she was past age, because she judged him faithful who had promised. Therefore sprang there even of one, and him as good as dead, so many as the stars of the sky in multitude, and as the sand which is by the sea shore innumerable. These all died in fatih, not having received the promises, but having seen them far off, and were persuaded of them, and embraced them, and confessed that they were strangers and pilgrims of the earth.

This is referred to as the faith hall of fame. The saints of old were not saved by works just as we are not. They were saved by faith just as we are saved by faith. All of the sacrifices, all of the rituals, all of the laws, the entire Old

Testament was to prepare them for the coming King! They knew this by seeing it in the making. "They died in faith." That means they are all in heaven now. They went to heaven based on their faith! The promise is the new birth. They were all saved, but they did not have the Holy Spirit guiding them, living in them, and comforting them. They were not able to go to heaven until Christ paid the penalty of their sins. While they were waiting on their promise, they went to paradise in the heart of the earth (Matthew 27:50-53; Luke 16:22). There is no amount of works that can get you into heaven! There is only faith in Jesus Christ!

What Works Will Get You without a True Relationship with Christ

It doesn't matter how many works you have done if it is without having a relationship with Jesus it will get you no where. Matthew 7:22-23 says, "Many will say to me in that day, Lord, Lord, have we not prophesied in thy name? And in thy name have cast out devils? And in thy name done many wonderful works? And then will I profess unto them, I never knew you: depart from me, ye that work iniquity"

From the previous passage it is clear that it's pointless to do works without Christ's love in our hearts. No matter how many, how mighty, how glamorous the works you do, if he's not in your life, then you will not be saved. You should ask yourself, "Do I do works to glorify him, or do I do works to glorify myself?" Do you have a relationship with God? Do you produce fruits worthy of his name? When you die, will you rely on your works or on Calvary? Eternity is too long to spend in agony and regret.

> What doth it profit, my brethren, though a man say he hath faith, and have not works? Can faith save him? If a brother or sister be naked, and destitute of daily food, And one of you say unto them, Depart in peace, be ye warmed and filled; notwithstanding ye give them not those things which are needful to the body; what doth it profit? Even so faith, if it hath not works, is dead, being alone. Yea, a man may say, Thou hast faith, and I have works: shew me thy faith without thy works, and I will shew thee my faith by my works. Thou believest that there is one God; thou doest well: the devils also believe, and

tremble. But wilt thou know, O vain man, that faith without works is dead? (James 2:14–20)

By reading this at a glance, you may think that it contradicts Ephesians 2:8–9. Some believe if you are not actively front and center in the choir, preaching, going door to door, and handing out tracts, then you are not going to heaven or not as loved by God.

This passage actually complements what Paul says, "We are not saved by works." Verses 15 and 16 make it clear that if we are not helping those in need, we are not living the fruit of the spirit, "peace, love, and joy" (Galatians 5:22). He tells us what he expects from us as Christians. He tells us anytime we "visit the sick, feed the hungry, or visit those who are in prison," then we do it unto him (Matthew 25:35–40). When you do these things, people will know that you belong to Christ (Matthew 5:14).

Our faith is ever-growing. It starts off small, and as we grow in Christ, so does our faith. If we don't exercise our prayer lives, study Scripture, attend church, and help others, then our faith is not going to be very effective. Many people say that they have faith in God but do not show it. They treat others harshly and are selfish. Non-Christians are looking for reasons not to come to Christ. When they see our faith without works, it does not show them a loving Christ. All they see is envy, jealousy, anger, and wrath.

How many times have you heard people say that they believe in God and then see them not act like Christians? All people believe in something. Even atheists believe in something. You cannot look at the earth, animals, plants, and people and accept that there is no divine Creator (Romans 1:20). If God were to judge you based on your works, would you be able to say that you are bearing good fruits? Our salvation is not based on our works. Our works are evidence of our salvation. Never give a reason for people to reject Christ because of your attitude! True salvation produces true works.

Works Tell Us about Who God Is.

The Amplified brings this passage out nicely 2 Timothy 2:15 "Study and be eager and do your utmost to present yourself to God approved (tested by trial), a workman who has no cause to be ashamed, correctly analyzing and accurately dividing [rightly handling and skillfully teaching] the Word of Truth."

Paul is telling us to study. The Holy Spirit is revealing to us the importance of studying. If we dedicate ourselves to studying, then we will not be tossed to and from by every wind of doctrine (Ephesians 4:14). When we dig into the Word, we become learned in the Word. The more we attend church the more our faith increases (Romans 10:17). Then we can become prayer warriors. We cannot become soldiers for God without faith, and works build faith. As our faith increases, the more able we are to please him (Hebrews 11:6). When we study, we will find out more about who God is, how he operates, and how we can follow his Spirit.

Works Establish Our Thoughts.

If we are working for Christ he can change our thought pattern. Proverbs 16:3 "Commit thy works unto the Lord, and thy thoughts shall be established."

If you are committing sinful works, then you are going to have sinful thoughts. If you have sinful thoughts, you will never be established in life. God will guide us if we commit all that we are unto him. He has plans for us to succeed and prosper, plans to give us hope and a future (Jeremiah 29:11). But we have to follow him if we are going to be established by him. When we give our lives to him, we must do just that, completely give all that we are to him. We must work with our hands, set our minds to him, and commit ourselves to Jesus Christ as our prize (Romans 12:2; Philippians 3:14). The more places I give him in my life, the more he directs me. If you allow him to govern your life, you, too, will see more involvement from him in your life.

What Works Are Expected of Us?

We as Christians sometimes do not know what Christ expects from us as works. Matthew 25:31–40 says,

> When the Son of man shall come in his glory, and all the holy angels with him, then shall he sit upon the throne of his glory: And before him shall be gathered all nations: and he shall separate them one from another, as a shepherd divideth his sheep from the goats: And he shall set the sheep on his right hand, but the goats on the left. Then shall the King say unto them on his right hand, Come, ye blessed of my Father, inherit the kingdom

prepared for you from the foundation of the world: For I was an hungred, and ye gave me meat: I was thirsty, and ye gave me drink: I was a stranger, and ye took me in: naked, and ye clothed me: I was sick, and ye visited me: I was in prison, and ye came unto me. Then shall the righteous answer him, saying, Lord, when saw we thee an hungred, and fed thee? Or thirsty, and gave thee drink? When saw we thee a stranger, and took thee in? Or naked, and clothed thee? Or when saw we thee sick, or in prison, and came unto thee? And the King shall answer and say unto them, Verily I say unto you, Inasmuch as ye have done it unto one of the least of these my brethren, ye have done it unto me.

These are the works that he wants us to do—to give, to care, to love others just as he has loved us, and to preach the gospel to all people (Matthew 22:37–39; Mark 16:15; Romans 10:14; Galatians 2:20). If we do these works, all of the world will see the light of Christ through us and give him glory (Matthew 5:16). Those who do these works are considered sheep. These are the works that James was talking about. The goats are the ones who did nothing for the kingdom. They were lazy and fruitless. If you are truly saved, there is going to be a love in your heart for him and the lost. If you do not produce any good fruit, you are probably not saved. It's not the works that save you. Salvation produces works. If you cannot tell whether you are a goat or a sheep, neither can Christ. I would suggest that you fully devote your life to him.

Works Have to Be Done with Love!

1 Corinthians 13:1-3 (ESV) says, "If I speak in the tongues of men and of angels, but have not love, I am a noisy gong or a clanging cymbal. And if I have prophetic powers, and understand all mysteries and all knowledge, and if I have all faith, so as to remove mountains, but have not love, I am nothing. If I give away all I have, and if I deliver up my body to be burned, but have not love, I gain nothing."

It doesn't matter what gift you have, no matter if you speak in the language of angels (tongues) or can prophesy. Even if you have the faith to move mountains, feed the poor, visit the sick, or help strangers, all of these things are done in vain if they are without love. Works must be backed with love because love is how others can tell that Christ lives in us. Our salvation is proved by our love for him. Our love for him is demonstrated to those around us. No one wants to come to Christ if his followers are hateful, boastful, arrogant, or rude. Love is the greatest commandment (Matthew 22:37–40).

Ask yourself if there is love or hatred in your heart when you do things for others. Examine your heart. Is there love in it? If you are a preacher, is the love coming out in your message, or is there pride, arrogance, and competition in your preaching? We must put our focus on love. If we do, then our gifts will become powerful tools. Love is the backbone to creation, redemption, and proclaiming the gospel!

What Do Works Earn Us?

Some denominations teach us that everyone gets the same reward in heaven whether you have served God faithfully or you get into heaven by the hair of your chin. That is true. If you are faithful to God with whatever gift he has given, the reward will be the same. If you think that because you are a preacher with a congregation of ten thousand people and you are puffed up with pride and self-righteousness and are also competitive with others, if you think that the people called to the help ministry (the ones who vacuum the church, take care of the nursery, etc.) are less important than you, then there may be a great surprise when God is passing out rewards. Really you should ask yourself if you know who God is!

"And, behold, I come quickly; and my reward is with me, to give to every man according to his work shall be" (Revelation 22:12).

God is going to reward us according to how we have handled the gifts he has given us (Matthew 25:14–30). If you were lazy with your gift, do not expect him to say, "Well done, good and faithful servant." Always remember that when you do good deeds for others but do not get paid for them, that does not mean the acts went unnoticed. God notices all deeds good and bad. We have one life to live. Even though we accept Christ as our Savior, that does not mean the work is over. It means that our heavenly job has just begun. We have a very short time here on earth to build up rewards in heaven and to bring as many to heaven as we can. I hope that you take the time to please God in this life.

According to the grace of God which is given unto me, as a wise master builder, I have laid the foundation, and another buildeth thereon. But let every man take heed how he buildeth thereupon. For other foundation can no man lay than that is laid, which is Jesus Christ. Now if any man build upon this foundation gold, silver, precious stones, wood, hay, stubble; every man's work shall be made manifest: for the day shall declare it, because it shall be revealed by fire; and the fire shall try every man's work of what sort it is. If any man's work abide which he hath built thereupon, he shall receive a reward. If any man's work shall be burned, he shall suffer loss: but he himself shall be saved; yet so as by fire. (1 Corinthians 3:10–15)

This passage tells us that we will still be saved from hell, but we will lose our rewards for the pride we have had and the way we have handled the gospel, of which he has made us stewards. We will see how we will be rewarded for handling the gifts that he has given us. If pride or laziness is our problem as Christians then our rewards will burn up like wood hay, and stubble because God opposes pride. When there is pride in our lives, he takes away our rewards (1 Peter 5:5). What do you truly have to be prideful for? He owns the cattle on a thousand hills. He owns everything in the earth. He can give and take away as he pleases.

> Beware of practicing your righteousness before other people in order to be seen by them, for then you will have no reward from your father who is in heaven. Thus, when you give to the needy, sound no trumpet before you, as the hypocrites do in the Synagogues and in the streets, that they may be praised by others. Truly, I say to you they have received their reward. But when you give to the needy, do not let your left hand know what your right have is doing, so that your giving may be in secret. And your father who sees in secret will rewards you. (Matthew 6:1–4 ESV)

Too many times we have done something for someone only to tell others about what we have done for them. We have all been guilty of that. But God doesn't intend for us to boast about what we do for one another. I have seen preachers who are pastors of large churches that are in competition with one another. This does not earn rewards for us. This only destroys what they could be earning. We must always stay humble. If you are a minister of a church, remember that one day you will be judged based on how you handle what gifts he has entrusted you with. Just because your congregation is large, that does not mean you are being rewarded. God may be testing you.

The Law

This is the Law. It explains God's standards for living. It was given to Moses on Mount Sinai after the Jews received their freedom from Pharaoh in Egypt. It was to show them what he expected from them, guidance for daily living, hygiene practices, how high his standards are, the penalty of sin, how expensive sin was, and the fact that we could not reach God.

The Ten Commandments

Exodus 20:1–17 says,

> And God spake all these words, saying, I am the LORD thy God, which have brought thee out of the land of Egypt, out of the house of bondage. Thou shalt have no other gods before me. Thou shalt not make unto

thee any graven image, or any likeness of anything that is in heaven above, or that is in the earth beneath, or that is in the water under the earth: thou shalt not bow down thyself to them, nor serve them: for I the LORD thy God am a jealous God, visiting the iniquity of the fathers upon the children unto the third and fourth generation of them that hate me; And shewing mercy unto thousands of them that love me, and keep my commandments. Thou shalt not take the name of the LORD thy God in vain; for the LORD will not hold him guiltless that taketh his name in vain. Remember the sabbath day, to keep it holy. Six days shalt thou labour, and do all thy work: But the seventh day is the sabbath of the LORD thy God: in it thou shalt not do any work, thou, nor thy son, nor thy daughter, thy manservant, nor thy maidservant, nor thy cattle, nor thy stranger that is within thy gates: For in six days the LORD made heaven and earth, the sea, and all that in them is, and rested the seventh day: wherefore the LORD blessed the sabbath day, and hallowed it. Honour thy father and thy mother: that thy days may be long upon the land which the LORD thy God giveth thee. Thou shalt not kill. Thou shalt not commit adultery. Thou shalt not steal. Thou shalt not bear false witness against thy neighbour. Thou shalt not covet thy neighbour's house, thou shalt not covet thy neighbour's wife, nor his manservant, nor his maidservant, nor his ox, nor his ass, nor any thing that is thy neighbour's.

This is the beginning of God's laws, which are referred to as the Ten Commandments. God gave them to the Israelites to teach them how to live, how to treat others, and ultimately how to worship him.

Notice he says, "I am the Lord thy God which have brought thee out of the land of Egypt, out of the house of bondage." He's telling Moses that he is God and reminding him of his power and reiterating the fact that he brought them out of the bondage. People are still being delivered from bondage. I am glad that Christ has delivered me from bondage. I may not have been in bondage to man, but I was in bondage to sin. Are you still subject to the bondage of the world and its sin? Or has God set you free? The payment for your salvation has been paid. If you haven't accepted it, you need to.

First Commandment

The first commandment says, "Thou shalt have no other Gods before me." This is the same commandment that Christ gave us in the New Testament (Luke 10:27-28). Why is it so important? It is important because Jesus is the only way to the Father and no man comes to the Father but by him (John 14:6). In other words, no one can get to heaven except through Jesus. This is a clear picture that shows he only accepts first place in our lives. Is he the first priority in your life, or is he nothing more than a holiday convenience?

Second Commandment

The second commandment says, "Thou shalt not make unto thee any graven image, or any likeness of anything that is in the heavens above, or that is in the earth beneath, or that is in the water under the earth. Thou shalt not bow down to them, nor serve them, for I the lord thy God am a jealous God."

God is making it known that we are not to worship any graven image. The Hebrew translation for graven is "carved images." This includes statues of Buddha, statues of Mary, and even a statue of Jesus. Yes! You may ask, "How can worshipping a statue of Jesus violate his commands?" Why would you want to worship a man-made image when you can worship the living God? We are to worship him in psalms, hymns, and spiritual songs (Ephesians 5:19; Colossians 3:16). We are to worship him also in spirit and truth (John 4:24). God gave us ways to worship him. It is okay to have a cross in your home or wear one around your neck or hang pictures of him. But we do not worship images or pray to them, we only worship our Lord.

Third Commandment

The third commandment says, "Thou shalt not take the name of the Lord thy God in vain." So many people say they don't believe in God, but they are quick to use his name as a curse word. When was the last time you heard someone curse Buddha or Allah when they stumped their toe or smashed a finger? They know his name is real.

That is why they are so quick to accuse him or curse him for their problems. We are only meant to use his name in praying, worshipping, and witnessing.

How many times have you claimed to be a follower of Christ? Instead you continue to live in sin? Do people have a hard time trying to distinguish you from a sinner? You may even have a hard time distinguishing yourself from a sinner. Yet you claim to be a Christian. People look at you and say, "Why would I want to be a Christian when he acts like me? If he is going to heaven, then so am I." This is how nonbelievers think when they see Christians who act no different than them. How can we expect to bring our loved ones to Christ if we cannot even show them the love of Christ in our lives?

We are to take on the title of his ambassador (2 Corinthians 5:20). We should always behave as such when we tell people we are followers of him. When you claim to be a Christian but act like a sinner, then you are taking his name in vain! We may be the only Bible some will ever read. Live it out the best you can!

Fourth Commandment

The fourth commandment says, "Remember the Sabbath day to keep it Holy." The Sabbath day was designed for man (Mark 2:27). People were to dedicate a portion of the week to God just as they were to dedicate a portion of their income to God (Malachi 3:10). It was also a day of rest. Rest is an important part of living a productive life. Without rest we are overworked, stressed, and tired. The servants and cattle were commanded to rest. Yes, even cattle, because he is Lord of all. Christ even took time for leisure from his ministry (Mark 6:30–31). Now we not only worship at church, but we worship every day because he is the Sabbath. It does not matter what day we worship him (Colossians 2:16). I have attended church services on Saturday, Tuesday, and Thursday basically every day, not just on Sundays. When you tell someone that you are attending a church service that does not fall on Sunday or Wednesday, they act as if you belong to a cult. Whether it is Sunday or Monday, it is of no significance as long as we do not forsake the assembly (Hebrews 10:25).

Fifth Commandment

The fifth commandment says, "Honor thy father and thy mother and thy days maybe long upon the land which the lord gives thee."

People want to eat healthy, take vitamins, and exercise to increase their life span, but they often fail to respect their parents. They get what they can out of them, and that's all they want. These people are less concerned for their parents and more concerned about themselves. Teenagers do what they want. They all too often disrespect their parents. They fail to realize that their parents want good things for them (Matthew 7:9–11). We have a lot to learn from our parents. That is why God gave them to us. We should love them and respect them, especially as they get older.

Sixth Commandment

The sixth commandment says, "Thou shalt not kill." Murder is very wrong. It affects the victim, the families of the victim, even the taxpayers. But God looks at the heart. There does not have to be a physical death for murder to occur. Christ tells us that anger and hate are the same as murder (Matthew 5:21–26). Have you ever been angry with a person or hated someone? Everyone at one point or another has murdered someone in his or her heart. Anger can build to the point of murder. We should not be so quick to judge or convict people who have murdered others. After all, we are all murderers in our hearts, sinners saved by grace.

Seventh Commandment

The seventh commandment says, "Thou shalt not commit adultery." Adultery affects everyone—husband, wife, and children. Adultery brings confusion, disease, hate, anger, stress, and sometimes even murder. When they brought out the woman who was caught in the act of adultery, she was about to be stoned. Christ wrote something in the sand and told them, "He who has not sinned cast the first stone," and they all left (John 8:7). I believe he wrote all their sins in the sand for everyone to see. Christ came to offer forgiveness of sins, not punishment. That is why he rode on a donkey. It represented peace (John 12:12–16). When he returns, he will be riding on a horse, representing war (Revelation 19:11–16).

Some couples have an open relationship. That is a nice way of saying, "My spouse is not enough for me to stay happy, so we give each other permission to cheat."

God gave one man to one woman. They became one flesh (Matthew 19:5; Ephesians 5:31). Marriage is meant to be between one man and one woman, not between a man and another man or between two women. It is not meant to be trampled on by open relationships. Sometimes the Devil will put lustful thought in our minds. Just rebuke them in the name of Jesus and turn them over to God. That way if the situation ever presents itself, you will be able to handle it because you have dealt with it in your heart, so it will not manifest in the flesh.

Eighth Commandment

The eighth commandment says, "Thou shalt not steal." People work very hard for the things they have, and when others steal from them, it shows how lazy these thieves are. I have had vehicles stolen (more than once). I have had things stolen from our hunting club (more than once). My dad has had his guns stolen (more than once). When things are stolen, it causes anger and sometimes hatred. It can lead to death if the family is home when the robber breaks in. I know myself. If someone broke into my home while I was there, I would not hesitate to use deadly force. You think I am wrong? I would not be wrong to protect my family. The bible says, "If a thief is found breaking in and is struck so that he dies, there shall be no blood guilt for him" (Exodus 22:2 ESV). Always protect your family, yourself, and your belongings.

Ninth Commandment

The ninth commandment says, "Thou shalt not bear false witness." This commandment means that we should not indulge in lies, half-truth, or manipulations. How many people have lied in the hopes of changing the outcome in their favor? This has probably been the reason for a lot of wrongful death and perhaps years spent in prison because of bearing false witness. Have you ever known anyone who lied against a fellow employee to get recognition or promotion? My mother once worked at a nursing home, and while she was working there, her husband got sick and had to be hospitalized. She asked a coworker to cover for her during her lunch break while she went to check on him (the hospital was close by) just in case it took longer than the time allotted for her break. The coworker agreed but then filed a grievance report, and my mother was fired. Her coworker lied in hopes of obtaining a promotion. Lies destroy friendships, families, marriage, and trust.

Tenth Commandment

The final commandment reads, "Thou shalt not covet thy neighbor's house, thou shalt not covet thy neighbor's wife, nor his man servant, nor his maid servant, nor his ox, nor his ass, nor anything that is thy neighbors."

We do not need to dwell on other people's possessions, whether it is your neighbor's home on the lake or the new sports car. There is nothing wrong with being successful. These people can tell us how God taught them to manage their finances with wisdom. These people can be very useful in our lives. We do not need to be greedy. Keeping up with the Jones's is our weakness here in America. We need to be more concerned with ourselves and less concerned with everyone else. Praise God for what others have and be thankful for what God has given to you.

Laws Concerning People

There are 613 laws. You will be glad to know that I have not listed all of them here. However, consider the following:

> "He that smiteth a man, so that he die, shall
> be surely put to death. And he that smiteth

his father and his mother shall be surely put to death. If men strive, and hurt a woman with child, so that her fruit depart from her, and yet no mischief follow: he shall be surely punished, according as the woman's husband will lay upon him; and he shall pay as the judges determine." (Exodus 21:12, 15, 22).

This begins with the punishment of men. The passage says, "He that smiteth a man so that he dies shall surely be put to death." This law still applies in most countries. "And he that smiteth his father or his mother shall surely be put to death" (Exodus 21:15). These are some of the basic laws concerning how to treat people.

Laws about Property and General Laws

Exodus 22:1–4 (ESV) says,

> If a man steals an ox or a sheep, and kills it or sells it, he shall repay five oxen for an ox, and four sheep for a sheep. If a thief is found breaking in and is struck so that he dies, there shall be no bloodguilt for him, but if the sun has risen on him, there shall

be bloodguilt for him. He shall surely pay. If he has nothing, then he shall be sold for his theft. If the stolen beast is found alive in his possession, whether it is an ox or a donkey or a sheep, he shall pay double.

Then Exodus 22:16–20 (ESV) says,

If a man seduces a virgin who is not betrothed and lies with her, he shall give the bride—price for her and make her his wife. If her father utterly refuses to give her to him, he shall pay money equal to the bride—price for virgins. You shall not permit a sorceress to live. Whoever lies with an animal shall be put to death. Whoever sacrifices to any god, other than the Lord alone, shall be devoted to destruction.

These are just a few laws. They are to lay down the foundation of a moral law to the Israelites. They covered building altars, doing things for priests, and procedures for worshipping and living. The laws explain about sacrifices, how to offer them, and what their purpose was. They also explain worship in feast and national holidays. There are laws about disease, directions for handling food, spiritual and physical principles, and laws about sex.

When God took his people out of Egypt, he also had to take Egypt out of the people. Egypt was sinful, so God gave the Israelites moral laws to follow.

The book of Leviticus discusses burnt offerings, grain offerings, peace offerings, sin offerings, guilt offerings, clean and unclean animals, rules about leprosy, sexual perversions, punishments for sin, standards for priests, commandments for daily life, feast for unleavened bread, and feast of firstfruits.

God's commandments would be broken again and again by his people. He sent prophets to warn them of judgment if they did not turn from their sinful ways. One of God's chosen men was a prophet named Jeremiah. Jeremiah was proclaiming a message from God about repentance. He knew the Israelites would not listen and the punishment would be severe. He stayed up throughout the night, crying himself to sleep because he knew the coming judgment that awaited them.

All this crying earned him the nickname "the weeping prophet." All of the worries and cares of the people's future judgment pushed him into weeping for them. He goes on to quote "My eyes are spent with weeping, my stomach churns; and my bile is poured out to the ground because of the destruction of the daughter of my people because infants and babies faint in the streets of the city" (Lamentation 2:11 ESV).

During the judgment while Israel was being handed over to Babylon, they actually turned cannibal (Jeremiah 19:9; Lamentation 4:10). That is how bad it got! Eventually the people became very zealous for God in fear of his judgment on them. How would you feel if you knew the fate of the ones you loved who refused to change their lifestyles and repent of their sins? What about the fate of the ones you know who are going to hell because they do not know Jesus? Does it make you weep knowing many will reject him? Does it make you weep knowing that many will go to hell?

Eventually the people grasped the concept that they could not serve idols and false gods. They followed the law so closely that they added to it. They called these additions the "traditions of the elders." When Christ came here to serve the people and preach that the kingdom was at hand, the leaders and many others refused him because of the hardness of their hearts. Eventually they crucified him. If they had paid attention to the Holy Scripture, they would have known what to expect from the Messiah. The Old

Testament Scripture told of the lineage he would come from and the miracles he would perform. He was the only candidate who could fulfill the Scripture. He was a perfect match. The Old Testament is the New Testament concealed, while the New Testament is the Old Testament revealed. Peter was the first person to ever receive the revelation of this. We call it the "great confession" (Matthew 16:13–19).

Other Reasons the Law Was Given to the Israelites

The law is given to us by God through Moses. It is a perfect law because it was given by God. The psalmist tells us, "The law of God is in his heart; none of his steps shall slide" (Psalm 37:31). This law was to keep man from taking the wrong direction. It is thought of as a guide for everyday living. Even though we do not live by the Old Testament law, we do live by the commandments that Christ gave us. God has commanded us to love him first and our neighbor secondly. The Ten Commandments are good for us as a check to make sure our morals are in line with God's standards.

"The law of the Lord is perfect, reviving the soul: the testimony of the Lord is sure making wise the simple" (Psalm 19:7 ESV). The law makes wise the simple. God uses the people who are simple to the world and makes them wise. God does not just call the wise, perfect, noble, and rich (1 Corinthians 1:26). He chooses the weak and makes them strong (1 Corinthians 1:27; 2 Corinthians 12:9). The world looks at the simple and our weakness. But God's weakness is stronger than men's strength, and the foolishness of God is wiser than the wisest man. This is to show how mighty our Creator is. In our weakness we can overcome hard times by faith in Jesus Christ. Then a testimony is born.

"The law of the Lord is perfect, converting the soul" (Psalm 19:7). The law turns people to Christ, and it helps keep us in check by giving sinners a set of God's standards. Even though we are no longer under the law (Romans 10:4), we are under his grace.

"For sin shall no longer be your master because you are not under the law, but under Grace" (Romans 6:14 NIV). This passage makes it clear that the law and sin are synonymous. You may ask how the law and sin are the same since God created the law. Does that mean that God is sin? God is sinless. He defines what sin in. The law could never remove sin. Only Christ's blood can remove the burden of sin. The law constantly points out our sin. If we try to justify ourselves according to the law, which points out every sin that we have committed in the past, we are found to be sinners. The main purpose of the law is to point out that we are sinners in need of an ultimate sacrifice, someone who can pay the price for all the sins in our lives.

Now we are under grace, which is our new covenant issued by the blood of Christ and reconciled to the Father for us (2 Corinthians 5:18; Colossians 1:20). Many of our laws come from the Old Testament. These keep us humble because we constantly measure ourselves to God's standards. They convict the lost for their sins by helping them understand that their lives have failed God's standards. When they have acknowledged God's standards, they will realize their desperate need for him. Ask yourself, "Have I broken any of God's laws?" The answer is yes! You are guilty of sin! "For all have sinned, and come short of the glory of God " (Romans 3:23). The wages of sin are death, both physical death and spiritual death (Romans 6:23). But reconciliation is only a prayer away!

God's Word tells us that we all have sinned (Romans 3:23). Since no one could fulfill the law, God sent someone who could (Matthew 5:17). By his Son's obedience here on earth, he was the only one who had never sinned. Under submission to the Father, he was obedient even unto death

(Romans 5:19; Philippians 2:8). Since Christ was the only one not under the curse of sin and able to keep the law, he was the only one who could take on our sins. A slave cannot purchase another slave. Only a free man can purchase a slave. We were all slaves to the law of sin. But Christ came and was obedient and completely sinless. He was a free man, and he paid the bail bondsman for you! You now have the ability in Christ to live free! That is why only he could be the perfect sacrifice for our sins. He was the only who could purchase freedom for us.

Do Some Churches Still Operate under the Law?

Yes! Many churches operate under the law, which is considered legalism. Some operate under Old Testament laws by only worshipping on Saturdays and only eating certain things. And some churches make up their own laws and standards to dominate the church instead of allowing the Holy Spirit to guide and teach (Mark 7:13; Colossians 2:8). The laws of man hinder the Spirit and do not produce unity or bring about the fruit of the Spirit (Ephesians 4:11–16, 30; Galatians 5:22–23; 1 Thessalonians 5:19). Living under man's laws for the church brings out the big I's and little you's in their assembly. True unity cannot be established in those churches. The church is supposed to be unified by love and the gifts of the Holy Spirit. Many of man's interpretations are not in harmony with God's Word. We need to study the Bible daily as a handbook to daily living in and out of the church.

> Knowing that a man is not justified by the works of the law, but by the faith of Jesus Christ, even we have believed in Jesus Christ, that we might be justified by the faith of Christ, and not by the works of the law: for by the works of the law shall no flesh be justified. But if, while we seek to be justified by Christ, we ourselves also are found sinners, is therefore Christ the minister of sin? God forbid. For if I build again the things which I destroyed, I make myself a transgressor. For I through the law am dead to the law, that I might live unto God. I am crucified with Christ: nevertheless I live; yet not I, but Christ liveth in me: and the life which I now live in the flesh I live by the faith of the Son of God, who loved me, and gave himself for me. I do not frustrate the grace of God: for

if righteousness come by the law, then Christ
is dead in vain. (Galatians 2:16–21)

All we have to do is believe in our hearts and confess
with our mouths that Christ is our Savior (Romans 10:9).
Scripture does not say that we just need to believe it. It
says that we must also confess it. When you speak with
your mouth that he is God, confession is made. That is all
you must do to. You do not need to be baptized to receive
him into your life, you don't need to go door-to-door, you
do not have to do anything to receive a free gift which is
salvation!

The Law Is Still Good.

First Timothy 1:8–11 (ESV) says,

> Now we know that the law is good, if one
> uses it lawfully, understanding this that the
> law is not laid down for the just but for the
> lawless and disobedient, for the ungodly
> and sinners, for the unholy and profane, for
> those who strike their fathers and mothers,
> for murderers, the sexually immoral, men
> who practice homosexuality, enslavers, liars,

perjurers, and whatever else is contrary to sound doctrine, in accordance with the gospel of the glory of the blessed God, with which I have been entrusted.

Although we are not to justify ourselves by the law, it does not keep us in right standings with God. Nor does it keep us from hell. The law is good, meaning that it is holy if one uses it *lawfully*. It is not meant to dominate, to abuse, or to gain authority over others. It is meant to reveal sin.

This passage is an indicator that the law is for the lost. As previously stated, it gives a guideline for moral living. Ultimately it shows sinners that they do not match God's standards. These sinners are called out accordingly— homosexuality, murder, and sexual immorality. The sin is completely revealed to them by the law not only in the Ten Commandments but also in the rest of the law. If you are flesh and blood, then you have broken some laws. Homosexuals say, "God is love," and we "love one another." True, God is love. He loves us, and we are supposed to love one another. That's the two commandments that Christ left us with. Homosexuality is wrong, but there is hope in obtaining a new life with Christ (2 Corinthians 5:17). If you read the passage, you see that homosexuality is not even at the top of the list of sins. The profane and the ones who strike their fathers are listed above the sin of homosexuality. How do you treat your parents? Do you honor them and respect them, or do you treat them as criminals?

The Greatest Commandment

Christ gave two specific commandments that we need in our lives. They answer all of the problems we face in our lives, marriages, relationships with our coworkers, families, etc., and they give us more abundant lives physically and spiritually.

> But when the Pharisees had heard that he had put the Sadducees to silence, they were gathered together. Then one of them which was a lawyer, asked him a question, tempting him, saying, Master, which is the great commandment in the law? Jesus said unto him, Thou shalt love the Lord thy God with all thy heart, and with all thy soul, and with all thy mind. This is the first and great commandment. And the second is like unto it, Thou shalt love thy neighbour as thyself.

On these two commandments hang all the
law and the prophets. (Matthew 22:34–40)

These religious people tried to trick Jesus. When they
asked him which law was the greatest, the answer they
received was not as they expected. That is how intelligent
our Lord is. He always knows best. No matter what
situation you are going through, he has all the answers.
He handles our concerns with understanding, love, and
gentleness. All you must do is seek him. When we put him
first, we can have faith in him and trust in him.

If we loved our neighbors as ourselves, there would be
no stealing, murder, or cheating. Life would all be lived
in perfect harmony with one another. If we love Christ,
he will be active in our lives and give us the greatest gift
of all—eternal life. If we live by these principles, we can
turn the world upside down with the love of Christ. Do
you love Christ with all your heart, body, soul, and spirit?
Have you completely turned your life over to him? Or
are you just relying on him and loving him when it is
convenient for you? Do you love your family, friends,
coworkers, neighbors, and strangers? Or do they only feel
hate, jealousy, and selfishness coming from you?

Blood

In the Old Testament animals were sacrificed in order to cover sins. This is also why circumcision was needed. It was done to show that people were in a covenant with the almighty God. The sacrifice was for thanksgiving, praise, and the covering of sin. All this bloodshed was for a purpose. "And almost all things are by the law purged with blood; and without shedding of blood there is no remission of sins" (Hebrews 9:22). This is why we need a sacrifice. When a life is taken, it is taken in place of another so that the other may live. In other words, "a life for a life." The actual salvation was not purchased by the blood of animals. "For it is not possible that the blood of bulls and of goats should take away sins" (Hebrews 10:4). The purpose of the law and the sacrifices were to teach people the penalty of sin and to show them just how drastic their sin was through the expensive purchase of the animal. They were saved by faith in the blood just as we are saved by faith in the blood. They just couldn't be in God's presence until the debt was paid. They spent their time in Abraham's bosom (Luke 16:22). When Christ paid the price the Old Testament saints came up out of the ground (Matthew 27:50–53).

The First Bloodshed

Genesis 3:1–7 (ESV) says,

> Now the serpent was more crafty than any other beast of the field that the LORD God had made. He said to the woman, "Did God actually say, 'You shall not eat of any tree in the garden?" And the woman said to the serpent, "We may eat of the fruit of the trees in the garden, but God said, 'You shall not eat of the fruit of the tree that is in the midst of the garden, neither shall you touch it, lest you die.'" But the serpent said to the woman, "You will not surely die. For God knows that when you eat of it your eyes will be opened, and you will be like God, knowing good and evil." So when the woman saw

that the tree was good for food, and that it was a delight to the eyes, and that the tree was to be desired to make one wise, she took of its fruit and ate, and she also gave some to her husband who was with her, and he ate. Then the eyes of both were opened, and they knew that they were naked. And they sewed fig leaves together and made themselves loincloths.

This is exactly how Satan operates. "He is a roaring lion seeking whom he may devour" (1 Peter 5:8). He either attacks you himself, or he uses one of his demons to do it. Satan told Eve that if she ate of the fruit, she would be like God (Genesis 3: 5). He knew when she did that, the earth system would be handed over to him (Luke 4:6). He wanted to be god from the very beginning (Isaiah 14:14). That did not work out, so he tried his luck on humanity. He tries to tempt us and lure us away from God with the "lust of the flesh, lust of the eyes and the pride of life" (1 John 2:16). Satan comes to us with a promise of bigger and better ways in life. He masquerades himself as an angel of light (2 Corinthians 11:14). He does not appear as an old, ugly serpent. So when he comes to you, it will never be as anything ugly, but he'll offer something you think you cannot live without.

When Adam and Eve both ate the fruit, their eyes were opened (Genesis 3: 7). I wonder how many marriages have been destroyed because that good-looking man or woman who looked so good to the eyes and that spouse who was looking at the bigger, better deal gave in to the apple of their eye just as Adam and Eve did. Once they did, their eyes were opened. They felt naked because they knew they had done wrong before the Lord. At that moment when the Lord caught them red-handed, they realized that the few minutes of eating that fruit wasn't worth it. In the same way adultery in marriages is fun for a season. By the time the crime has been committed, the realty sets in.

When God came into the garden of Eden, Adam and Eve hid; because they were naked (Genesis 3:10). This shows just how innocent they were. They were just like children. I know my children as little toddlers. We could not keep clothes on them. They enjoyed their freedom and innocence. This is how God originally created us—free from shame, free form guilt, free from sins, and completely innocent. In many ways God wants is to be like our children. He even tells us to have faith as children and to be completely reliant on him.

God asked Adam how he knew he was naked, if he had eaten of the Tree of Knowledge, which was forbidden (Genesis 3:11)? Adam responded, "The woman you gave to be with me, she gave me fruit of the tree and I ate" (Geneses 3: 12). Apparently he shifted the blame to her. Really he blamed God by saying, "You gave her to me." I can just imagine how he was trying to get out of it. He must have been nervous. Too many times we are just like Adam, always blaming someone else for our mistakes.

Then God asked Eve, "What have you done?" Eve responded, "The serpent deceived me" (Geneses 3: 13). This reminds me of high school and family drama. It's the "he said, she said" type of drama. I think all too often we need to stand up and accept responsibility in our lives and realize there are consequences to our actions. The consequences for their disobedience resulted in the fall of humanity. Really it was the fall of everything. God's response to Eve was, "I will surely multiply your pain in child bearing, in pain you shall bring forth children. Your desire shall be for your husband, and he shall rule over you" (Genesis 3:16 ESV).

Genesis 3:17–19 then says,

> And unto Adam he said, Because you have hearkened unto the voice of thy wife, and hast eaten of the tree, of which I commanded thee, saying, Thou shalt not eat of it: cursed is the ground for thy sake; in sorrow shalt thou eat of it all the days of your life; thorns and thistles it shall bring forth to thee; and thou shalt eat the herb of the field. In the sweat of thy face you shall eat bread, till you return to the ground, for out of it wast thou taken: for dust thou art, and unto dust shalt thou return.

This is where all of the problems in the world originated. The only hope for them was a sacrifice to cover their sins and their bodies. So the Lord slew an animal to cover their bodies, using the skin of the animal and the blood as a sacrifice (Geneses 3:21).

You may think that eating fruit is no big deal. It's not the eating of the fruit. It's the simple act of his disobedience, or better stated, it is the act of rebellion. I have heard preachers say, "All those preachers who believe sin entered when Adam ate of the fruit are wrong." They believe it was because Adam would not repent. That is a total misunderstanding of the Scripture. Adam was told by God not to eat of the fruit, or else he would surely die! This was not a conditional warning. It was a promise. They disobeyed God. This disobedience was an act of sin, and "there is no remission of sin without blood" (Hebrews 9:22). Besides that Adam did repent when the animal was killed.

I believe that the Tree of Knowledge was more than what meets the eye. I believe it was a tithing tree. You may think to yourself that tithing was a part of the law and that the law had not yet been given. That is true. It was part of the law (Leviticus 27:32); however, Abraham paid tithes to Melchizedek (Hebrews 7:6). This was around five hundred to six hundred years before the law was given to Moses. Tithing is not just a practice of the law in the Old Testament. It is also a New Testament practice taught by Christ (Matthew 23:23; Luke 11:42).

You may ask how can you say that this was a tithing tree? Look at Cain and Abel's offerings. "And Abel was a keeper of sheep, but Cain was a tiller of the ground. And in process of time it came to pass that Cain brought of the first fruit of the ground and an offering unto the Lord. And

Abel he also brought of the first lings of his flock and of the fat there of. And the Lord had respect unto Abel and to his offering but unto Cain and to his offering he had not respect. And Cain was very wroth, and his countenance fell" (Genesis 4:2–5).

These two brothers (Cain and Abel) had different jobs. One tended animals, while the other was a farmer. They were both bringing offerings to the Lord, but one of those offerings was vegetables and fruit. This was not a sacrifice for sins. It was a tithe. But Cain was rejected by God when he brought his tithe to God. So why did God reject his offering? I think he did so because of his attitude. Tithing is a form of worship. I believe his heart was not right before God. His thinking was probably this: *Why do I have to give the best when I can keep it for myself? We are told to be cheerful givers (2 Corinthians 9:7).* If this was a tithe, then who taught them? Yes, it was Adam and Eve! This is why they couldn't eat of the tree. The whole earth was to be Adam's. He was to be Lord over it, and the tree was to be his worship unto the Lord so that he could remember where everything that had been given to him came from. When Adam and Eve stole from God, they were cursed (Genesis 3:17–19).

Genesis 3:11–19 says,

> And he said, Who told thee that thou wast naked? Hast thou eaten of the tree, whereof I commanded thee thou shouldest not eat? And the man said, The woman whom thou gavest to be with me, she gave of the tree, and I did eat. And the Lord God said unto the woman, What is this that thou hast done? And the woman said, The serpent beguiled me, and I did eat. And the Lord God said unto the serpent, Because thou hast done this, thou art cursed above all cattle, and above every beast of the field; upon thy belly shalt thou go and dust shalt thou eat all the days of thy life: and I will put enmity between thee and the woman, and between thy seed and her seed; it shall bruise thy head, and thou shalt bruise his heel. Unto the woman he said, I will greatly multiply thy sorrow and thy conception; in sorrow thou shalt bring forth children; and thy desire shall be to thy husband, and he shall rule over thee. And unto Adam he said, Because

thou hast hearkened unto the voice of thy wife, and hast eaten of the tree, of which I commanded thee, saying, Thou shalt not eat of it: cursed is the ground for thy sake; in sorrow shalt thou eat the herb of the field; in the sweat of thy face shalt thou eat bread, till thou return unto the ground; for out of it wast thou taken: for dust thou art, and unto dust shalt thou return.

Malachi 3:8–12 also says,

Will a man rob God? Yet ye have robbed me. But ye say, Wherein have we robbed thee? In tithes and offerings. Ye are cursed with a curse: for ye have robbed me, even this whole nation. Bring ye all the tithes into the storehouse, that there may be meat in mine house, and prove me now herewith, saith the Lord of hosts, if I will not open you the windows of heaven, and pour you out a blessing, that there shall not be room enough to receive it. And I will rebuke the devourer for your sakes, and he shall not destroy the fruits of your ground; neither shall your vine cast her fruit before the time in the field, saith the Lord of hosts. And all nations shall call you blessed: for ye shall be a delightsome land, saith the Lord of hosts.

Do you see the comparison? Adam and Eve were blessed until they stole from God. They were blessed if they gave to God and cursed if they stole from God. Although we are no longer cursed for not tithing because "Christ hath redeemed us from the curse of the law, being made a curse: for it is written, cursed is everyone that hangeth on a tree" (Galatians 3:13). Even thou we are not cursed as they were since Christ took the curse to the cross for us. Obedience to tithing still brings blessings to those who obey. When we choose to keep the tithes, we are saying, "I don't trust God with my finances, and I choose to follow Satan and trust him with them" (Luke 16: 10-13).

Adam taught Cain and Abel to tithe, and they in turn taught their descendants, who taught Abraham long before God gave the law to Moses. We should follow their footsteps in our giving. Tithing promotes the gospel (by funding it), and it releases blessings and opportunities that would not otherwise come to us. Most Christians do not tithe and thus would have broken God's commandment just as Adam. But there are other ways to disobey God.

Has God ever told you to do something that you didn't do? Have you always been faithful and gone to church? What about forgiving your friends and family? We have all done things we are not supposed to do. We have all been selfish. We have all sinned (Romans 3:23). You may say, "I am only human. Everyone makes mistakes." That is true, but we make those mistakes because of our inheritance of disobedience from Adam (Romans 5:12–20). That doesn't give us the reason to continue living that sinful lifestyle!

Some people blame sickness and disease on Adam. People say, "If I was in his place, I would not have done what Adam did." It is true that he is the figurehead of the human race. It is also true that we all have broken God's laws and that all men and women would have disobeyed. God commanded us to love him with every part of us and to love our neighbors as ourselves and to forgive one another (Matthew 6:14; 22:37–40). We as Christians all too often fail to obey his commands. As a result, a sacrifice had to be made. This was going to be the first of many sacrifices to come. When God created Adam and Eve, he made them perfect in every way. They were physically strong and intelligent enough to name the animals of the field. Man lost all this and allowed sin to enter into the world by one act of disobedience.

Why Would God Ask Someone to Sacrifice His or Her Son?

Genesis 22:1–18 says,

> And it came to pass after these things, that God did tempt Abraham, and said unto him, Abraham. And he said, Behold, here I am. And he said, Take now thy son, thine only son Isaac, whom thou lovest, and get thee into the land of Moriah; and offer him there for a burnt offering upon one of the mountains which I will tell thee of. And Abraham rose up early in the morning, and saddled his ass, and took two of his young men with him, and Isaac his son, and clave the wood for the burnt offering, and rose up, and went unto the place of which God had told him. Then on the third day Abraham lifted up his eyes, and saw the place afar off. And Abraham said unto his young men, Abide ye

here with the ass; and I and the lad will go yonder and worship, and come again to you. And Abraham took the wood of the burnt offering, and laid it upon Isaac his son; and he took the fire in his hand, and a knife; and they went both of them together. And Isaac spake unto Abraham his father, and said, My father: and he said, Here am I, my son. And he said, Behold the fire and the wood: but where is the lamb for a burnt offering? And Abraham said, My son, God will provide himself a lamb for a burnt offering: so they went both of them together. And they came to the place which God had told him of; and Abraham built an altar there, and laid the wood in order, and bound Isaac his son, and laid him on the altar upon the wood. And Abraham stretched forth his hand, and took the knife to slay his son. And the angel of the Lord called unto him out of heaven, and said, Abraham, Abraham. And he said, here am I. And he said, lay not thine hand upon the lad, neither do thou anything unto him: for now I know that thou fearest God,

seeing thou hast not withheld thy son, thine
only son from me.

Abraham and Sarah had a hard time conceiving their
son. God came to them and told Abraham—at the time
his name was Abram—that "he would be a father and a
father to many nations." He had to introduce himself as a
father of many nations even though he was well stricken in
age and childless. He and Sarah wanted to help God out,
so he took his handmaiden, Hagar, and lay with her. She
conceived a son she named Ishmael. Sarah did not believe
she could bear children at her age. But God had a plan for
her. He said she would bear children, and that is what he
meant.

An angel of the Lord came unto Sara to inform her that
indeed she would bear a child. When she heard this, she
laughed because she doubted God (Genesis 18:12). How
many times have you doubted God? We all too often doubt
God. We do not need to doubt who God is. We just need
to enter into his rest (Matthew 11:28–30). Because Sarah
laughed at him, God instructed her to name her child Isaac,
which means *laughter.*

When people get the things they work hard for, they
love and appreciate them. Parents love their children. We

conceive them, feed them, and teach them. We become so attached to them that we would kill for them. The death of a child is traumatizing. How much more traumatizing would it be to have to sacrifice one of our own children.

Abraham and Sarah waited and waited for the day of their promised child to come. I can just imagine the tears of joy that rolled down their face when their baby boy came into the world. When I watched my firstborn come into the world, I was very excited. So why did God ask him to offer him as a sacrifice for sin in general. Ultimately God tested his faith and obedience. God wants us to love him above anyone and anything (Matthew 22:37). He even wants us to love him more than our own family (Matthew 10:37), because when your spouse has left you and your children are sinning you will always have a friend in Jesus that will never leave you. If we put him first in our own lives, everything else will follow (Matthew 6:33). God wants us to make sure he is the only God in our lives, for he is a jealous God (Exodus 20:5).

God had a promise to Abraham that he would bless him through Isaac, that the chosen nation would come, and that it would bless all mankind (Genesis 22:18). Abraham became the ancestor of Christ. When Abraham went to offer his son as a sacrifice, he did so knowing that God could raise him up from the ashes.

"By faith Abraham, when he was tried, offered up Isaac: and he that had received the promises offered up his only begotten son, Of whom it was said, That in Isaac shall thy seed be called: accounting that God was able to raise him up, even from the dead; from whence also he received him in a figure" (Hebrews 11:17–19).

This is the faith to move mountains. God wants us to walk by faith and not by sight. When things do not look possible to us, we need to have faith that with God all things are possible. As Abraham raised his hand with the knife, ready to drive it into Isaac with total faith in God that the Lord could raise him from the ashes, suddenly God stopped him! He presented him with a ram for a sacrifice. When Abraham seen the ram caught in the bushes I can just imagine the shouting and dancing that he did! God was pleased with Abraham. His works justified him because he put God first and acted on obedience. He is even mentioned in the faith hall of fame (Hebrews 11). He is also mentioned in the works hall of fame (James 2).

What a man of faith to be willing to go through this command. Because of his faith, he was blessed for his actions. God then made him the father of Israel. This is the type of men and women God needs, although God will not ask you to sacrifice a human life because he has already sacrificed himself. Has God ever asked you to sacrifice anything? Maybe he has asked you to give up tobacco and better provide for your family. Maybe he has asked you to give up drinking so that you can pay your bills. Maybe he asked you to stop going to night clubs. Maybe God has asked you to give up golfing or hunting on Sundays so you can get to know him better? God is willing to bless you in your life, but you must be willing to make sacrifices. The more room that you give to God in your life, the more he will move in.

What Is the Purpose of Circumcision?

Deuteronomy 10:12–16 says,

> And now, Israel, what doth the LORD thy God require of thee, but to fear the LORD thy God, to walk in all his ways, and to love him, and to serve the LORD thy God with all thy heart and with all thy soul, to keep the commandments of the LORD, and his statutes, which I command thee this day for

thy good? Behold, the heaven and the heaven of heavens is the LORD's thy God, the earth also, with all that therein is. Only the LORD had a delight in thy fathers to love them, and he chose their seed after them, even you above all people, as it is this day. Circumcise therefore the foreskin of your heart, and be no more stiff-necked.

This is the basic requirement that God expects from his people. They have changed much from then. He expects us to fear him (Psalm 115:11), to follow him (Psalm 1:1–3), and to love him with all our hearts (Matthew 22:37).

They were to circumcise their foreskin, but we are to circumcise our hearts (Romans 2:29; Philippians 3:3). Circumcision is a sign of a covenant between God and Israel. God told Abraham to circumcise his foreskin. He told him it would be a sign of a covenant between them (Genesis 17:11). The Hebrew word for circumcision is *namal,* and it means "to become clipped" or "to be cut off" (Strong #5243).

We no longer need to be circumcised to be in a covenant with God as Christians. We are to circumcise our hearts with the power of the new birth. By doing so, we will be filled with faith, hope, and love (1 Corinthians 13:13). This is the change that will take place on the inside. When we have changed on the inside, then there will be a change on the outside. This is how others will know that we are God's people.

Passover

Passover is when God was about to redeem his people from slavery in Egypt. Even in the middle of their hardship Jesus was still present with them just as he is present with you.

> Your lamb shall be without blemish, a male of the first year: ye shall take it out from the sheep, or from the goats: and ye shall keep it up until the fourteenth day of the same month: and the whole assembly of the congregation of Israel shall kill it in the evening. And they shall take of the blood, and strike it on the two side posts and on the upper door post of the houses, wherein they shall eat it. And thus shall ye eat it; with your loins girded, your shoes on your feet,

WHY MY BLOOD IS ENOUGH ✝

and your staff in your hand; and ye shall eat it in haste: it is the Lord's passover. For I will pass through the land of Egypt this night, and I will smite all the firstborn in the land of Egypt I will execute judgment: I am the Lord. And the blood shall be to you for a token upon the houses where ye are: and when I see the blood, I will pass over you, and the plague shall not be upon you to destroy you when I smite the land of Egypt. (Exodus 12:5-7, 11-13)

The Passover meal was designed to show appreciation for God, keeping people safe by passing over their homes during judgment. They were to do it quickly, ready with their shoes on their feet and staffs in hand (Exodus 12:11). God was about to lower the boom on Pharaoh, and he was going to be glad to get rid of the Israelites! While this judgment was coming, the people of Israel had to act in faith that God would save them from his wrath by putting lamb's blood on the door.

This lamb is what saved them from judgment. This blood of the sacrificed lamb is the same blood that will save us from the judgment to come. The lamb's blood was put on the doorpost. It was a sign of a covenant that their faith was in God. The same is true today. We are to mark ourselves with the blood of the Lamb (Jesus Christ). We do this to show God that we have faith in him through Jesus Christ and we believe that his covenant will save us from his wrath.

The lamb was to be a male, an archetype of Christ. It was to be without blemish (spotless). The lamb was to be perfect, not sick or blind. It couldn't have broken bones either (Deuteronomy 15:21). God did not accept anything less from Israel because he was a holy God worthy of all our praise and commitment. This type of lamb was expensive. It showed the people how expensive the cost of sin was. This is similar to paying a ticket or fine for breaking the law. Once we are found guilty, we are usually in shock of how expensive breaking the law is. Once we have paid the fine, there is a good chance that we will remember the penalty of the crime and avoid committing it again.

In the book of Malachi, God deals with the sin that the people were shorting him in tithes and sacrifices (offerings). They were disobedient to God in offerings and sacrifices. They were sacrificing the blind, lame, and sick (Malachi 1:8). But God said, "Cursed will be the ones who short hand me." God expected their best. He expects our best because he gave us his best (John 3:17). Passover is a perfect picture of how the blood of the lamb not only saved Israel from the wrath of God but will also save us.

Why Did God Command Different Sacrifices?

According to the *Strong's Exhaustive Concordance of the Bible*, sacrifice means "to slaughter an animal, to kill." There are five different kinds of offerings they fulfill and five purposes: show God our praise to him, our commitment to him, our thankfulness to him and removal of our sin, the importance of these offerings are to demonstrate to us the severity of our sin and to ultimately teach the children of Israel that their promised King was coming (Jesus).

Burnt Offerings

Leviticus 1:2–4 says,

> Speak unto the children of Israel, and say unto them, if any man of you bring an offering unto the LORD, ye shall bring your offering of the cattle, even of the herd, and of the flock. If his offering be a burnt sacrifice of the herd, let him offer a male

without blemish: he shall offer it of his own voluntary will at the door of the tabernacle of the congregation before the LORD. And he shall put his hand upon the head of the burnt offering; and it shall be accepted for him to make atonement for him.

The burnt offering made aroma to the Lord (Leviticus 1: 9, 13, and 15). It is intended to be a praise to God. Psalm 66:13–20 (ESV) then says,

I will come into your house with burnt offerings; I will perform my vows to you, that which my lips uttered and my mouth promised when I was in trouble. I will offer to you burnt offerings of fattened animals, with the smoke of the sacrifice of rams; I will make an offering of bulls and goats. Come and hear, all you who fear God, and I will tell what he has done for my soul. I cried to him with my mouth, and high praise was on my tongue. If I had cherished iniquity in my heart, the Lord would not have listened. But truly God has listened; he has attended

to the voice of my prayer. Blessed be God,
because he has not rejected my prayer or
removed his steadfast love from me!

David performed a burnt offering, and through the
passage we see that he was giving praise to God just as
a Noah did after the flood (Genesis 8:20–21). We made
sacrifices as gifts from us to God. They were given in
praise, worship, thanksgiving, forgiveness, and fellowship.

While David was performing his sacrifice, he was
praising God (Psalm 66: 17). He was letting us know that
if he had sinned, God would not have listened to him
(Psalm 66: 18). Sin keeps us from having fellowship with
God. We must constantly ask for forgiveness. God does
listen to you if you pray, but if you are a Christian, you
must keep repenting of your sins for your prayer life to be
effective. "If we confess our sins he is faithful and just to
forgive us of our sins" (1 John 1:9). If you have not given
your life to Christ, your prayers are not going to be heard
(John 9:31). We are not his children until we are born again
and embrace a covenant with him. Once we are born again,
our prayer lives are effective, but we must keep sin out of
our lives and do his will (James 5:16).

Grain Offerings

Leviticus 2:1-3 NIV says,

> When anyone brings a grain offering to the Lord, their offering is to be of the finest flour. They are to pour olive oil on it, put incense on it and take it to Aaron's sons the priests. The priest shall take a handful of the flour and oil, together with all the incense, and burn this as a memorial portion on the altar, a food offering, an aroma pleasing to the Lord. The rest of the grain offering belongs to Aaron and his sons; it is a most holy part of the food offerings presented to the Lord.

Grain offerings reminded people that their food came from God and they owed him their lives. There were three kinds of grain offerings—fine flour with oil and frankincense, baked cakes and wafers, and roasted kernels of corn with oil frankincense. Leaven was forbidden because it represented sin.

Some of the offerings were burned on the altar while the rest were consumed by the priest (Leviticus 2:10). Grain offering reminded the people that God was their provider.

He provides them with food, and they acknowledged him for it. As they burned it, the aroma satisfied him. It was not to have leaven in the offering (Leviticus 2:11). Yeast in the leaven is mold and fungus. It could grow to contaminate the rest of the bread. It is a perfect example of how sin spreads (1 Corinthians 5: 6-13). Sin in a marriage can grow too. Sin in a church can grow. This is why we as Christians should be separated from the world and we should be careful of who we spend our time with (Romans 12:2; 2 Corinthians 6:14; Ephesians 5:8, 11; 1 John 1:6, 7). "And every obligation of the meat offering shalt thy season with salt" (Leviticus 2:13). Salt represents God in our lives. He adds healing and seasons to our lives. Salt represents the Christian, or better stated, the Christian represents the salt (Matthew 5:13). Salt is also where we get the word salary from. Salt was once used as a form of payment because of its use and value. The average person ate grain with oil. It helped the people acknowledge God as the provider of their food. Have you ever wondered what you were going to eat or feed your family? Then God has moved on a loved one to provide for you or even a complete stranger to buy you groceries or give you money. Have you found money or been provided the extra work to feed your family? Does any of this sound familiar? If so, that was God providing for you. Give him thanks for all the times he provided for you!

Peace Offering

Leviticus 3:1–5 (ESV) says,

> If his offering is a sacrifice of peace offering, if he offers an animal from the herd, male or female, he shall offer it without blemish before the LORD. And he shall lay his hand on the head of his offering and kill it at the entrance of the tent of meeting, and Aaron's sons the priests shall throw the blood against the sides of the altar. And from the sacrifice of the peace offering, as a food offering to the LORD, he shall offer the fat covering the entrails and all the fat that is on the entrails, and the two kidneys with the fat that is on them at the loins, and the long lobe of the liver that he shall remove with the kidneys. Then Aaron's sons shall burn it on the altar on top of the burnt offering, which is on the wood on the fire; it is a food offering with a pleasing aroma to the LORD.

The peace offering was a way that the Israelites gave a thank-you as an expression of gratitude of having and maintaining fellowship between themselves and God. David gave a peace offering when he brought the Ark of the Covenant into the tent (1 Chronicles 16:2). Then David delivered psalms to the Lord. Our peace was laid on Christ at the cross. Through Christ you can now have peace with God and yourself by accepting his Son (Isaiah 53:5). You no longer have to make a sacrifice of peace offerings.

Sin Offering

Leviticus 4:3–8 says,

> If the priest that is anointed do sin according to the sin of the people; then let him bring for his sin, which he hath sinned, a young bullock without blemish unto the LORD for a sin offering. And he shall bring the bullock unto the door of the tabernacle of the congregation before the LORD; and shall lay his hand upon the bullock's head, and kill the bullock before the LORD. And the priest that is anointed shall take of the bullock's

blood, and bring it to the tabernacle of the congregation. And the priest shall dip his finger in the blood, and sprinkle of the blood seven times before the Lord, before the vail of the sanctuary. And the priest shall put some of the blood upon the horns of the altar of sweet incense before the Lord, which is in the tabernacle of the congregation; and shall pour all the blood of the bullock at the bottom of the altar of the burnt offering, which is at the door of the tabernacle of the congregation. And he shall take off from it all the fat of the bullock for the sin offering; the fat that covereth the inwards, and all the fat that is upon the inwards.

This offering is for priest who sins, which brings us to Christians who sin. God knew that you were going to sin before and after you received salvation. Our leaders in church sometimes sin. We say the wrong thing at the right time. Sometimes they mess up, get mad, and make mistakes. We should pray for them instead of holding everything that they have done wrong over their heads. If they continue to do wrong, take two or three witnesses with you. This is where deacons, elders, or church leaders who are open-minded come in handy. These people can help you confront the wrong others have committed. If that does not work, take the issue before the congregation or church. If the person still refuses to listen, let him be as if he was a sinner (Matthew 18:16, 17).

Leviticus 4:13–20 then says,

> And if the whole congregation of Israel sin through ignorance, and the thing be hid from the eyes of the assembly, and they have done somewhat against any of the commandments of the LORD concerning things which should not be done, and are guilty; when the sin, which they have sinned against it, is known, then the congregation shall offer a young bullock for the sin, and bring him before the tabernacle of the congregation. And the elders of the congregation shall lay their hands upon the head of the bullock before the LORD: and the bullock shall be killed before the LORD. And the priest that is anointed shall bring of the bullock's blood to the tabernacle of the congregation: and

the priest shall dip his finger in some of the blood, and sprinkle it seven times before the LORD, even before the veil. And he shall put some of the blood upon the horns of the altar which is before the LORD, that is in the tabernacle of the congregation, and shall pour out all the blood at the bottom of the altar of the burnt offering, which is at the door of the tabernacle of the congregation. And he shall take all his fat from him, and burn it upon the altar. And he shall do with the bullock as he did with the bullock for a sin offering, so shall he do with this: and the priest shall make atonement for them, and it shall be forgiven them.

People sin, and churches sin. We are all human beings. Humans sin. We all have broken his commandments. We all need a sacrifice that is large enough to clean us from our sins. Even our country has sinned as a whole. Look at the prisons filled with criminals. Some of the laws and mind-sets of people in America give more rights to animals than unborn children, and sex out of wedlock is accepted on television. When all this depravity is running rampant, we should know there is a moral problem in our country.

Reading God's Word (the Bible) will completely illuminate your thoughts and the intentions of your heart and show you just how sinful you are (Hebrews 4:12). It is powerful. It can change our lives not only as individuals but also as an entire nation (2 Chronicles 7:14). Being full of the Word will point out our sins and guide our lives. If people focused more on God, our prisons would not be so full.

Guilt Offering

Leviticus 5:14–16 says,

> And the LORD spake unto Moses, saying, If a soul commit a trespass, and sin through ignorance, in the holy things of the LORD; then he shall bring for his trespass unto the LORD a ram without blemish out of the flocks, with thy estimation by shekels of silver, after the shekel of the sanctuary, for a trespass offering. and he shall make amends for the harm that he hath done in the holy

thing, and shall add the fifth part thereto, and give it unto the priest: and the priest shall make an atonement for him with the ram of the trespass offering, and it shall be forgiven him. And if a soul sin, and commit any of these things which are forbidden to be done by the commandments of the Lord; though he wist it not, and it shall be forgiven him. It is a trespass offering: he has certainly trespassed against the Lord.

This offering is designed to take care of sins that we have committed without knowing it. This offering would need to be performed by all people if we were still under the old covenant. This sacrifice is for those who have sinned unintentionally against other people to restore them their loss plus 20 percent. How many times have you sinned against your neighbors, family members, coworkers, and friends? I do not know one person who has been perfect all the time. When people borrow money or items, they usually do not repay the money or return the items. What if we had to repay an extra 20 percent? That would make people respect property of others a little more.

The Last Supper

Matthew 26:26–29 says,

> And as they were eating, Jesus took bread,
> and blessed it, and brake it, and gave it to
> the disciples, and said, Take, eat; this is my
> body. And he took the cup, and gave thanks,
> and gave it to them, saying, Drink ye all of
> it; for this is my blood of the new testament,
> which is shed for many for the remission
> of sins. But I say unto you, I will not drink
> henceforth of this fruit of the vine, until that
> day when I drink it new with you in my
> Father's kingdom.

This is the Last Supper Christ had with his disciples.
The Last Supper was held on Passover, which was meant
to celebrate how God saved his people from judgment and
from Pharaoh. Those who had wiped the blood of the
lamb on their doorposts were saved (Exodus 12:7, 22).
The bread that they broke and ate was that of the Lamb
(Matthew 26:26; Mark 14:22; Luke 22:19; 1 Corinthians
11:24). When they were with Christ at the Last Supper,
he clearly explained to them that the Passover meal

represented his body. Jesus goes on to explain that his blood is for the remission of sins (Matthew 26:28; Luke 22:20; 1 Corinthians 11:25). Nowhere did he say that his blood was not enough for the remission of sins. He clearly stated that his blood and his blood alone is for the remission of sins. The blood that he shed issued a new and better Covenant (Hebrews 10:9–10), one that would allow all saved men and women to approach God through Jesus Christ to obtain help in time of need (1 Timothy 2:5; Hebrews 4:16). If we believe that his blood is not enough to save us from our sins, then we make the Bible out to be a liar.

We are still to partake in the Last Supper. "And when he had given thanks, he brake it, and said, Take, eat: this is my body, which is broken for you: this do in remembrance of me. After the same manner also he took the cup, when he had supped, saying, this cup is the new testament in my blood: this do ye, as oft as ye drink it, in remembrance of me" (1 Corinthians 11; 24, 25). We do this in remembrance of him. Some took the Communion with no respect for what Christ did for us, and they dropped dead (1 Corinthians 11:29-30). When we are taking Communion, we need to always take it seriously and with respect. If we disrespect

Communion, then we disrespect the sacrifice he made for us. Communion is a sacred ceremony just as baptism is.

The Ultimate Sacrifice

"The next day John seeth Jesus coming unto him, and saith, behold the Lamb of God, which takeh away the sin of the world" (John 1:29).

Jesus is the Lamb of God, the Passover lamb. He is the only one who can take away our sins. There are three important points from the previously mentioned passage. The first is that Jesus is the Lamb (Old Testament and New Testament). The next is that he takes our sins away. The last is that there is nothing we must add to his sacrifice to take away our sins. His blood is enough to remove all sins past, present, and future.

God humbled himself to the form of a servant. He was obedient in his life here on earth until his death (Philippians 2:7, 8). He took our rightful place on the cross, which we should have taken. He took on our punishment. How amazing is it that he gave his life so that we may live! He laid down his life for you! Now we can have everlasting life! No other God has ever accomplished that. This makes him the only true God.

When Christ was hanged on the cross, he made a statement. He said, "Father, why have you forsaken me?" (Matthew 27:46; Mark 15:34). This is when all of our sins past, present, and future were laid on him. Everything that you have ever said, did, or thought about was laid on him at that moment! He was a spotless lamb that had never sinned (1 Peter 1:19). He had to be spotless. Only something clean can remove something dirty. Another statement made from the cross was, "It is finished" (John 19:30). At that time the prophecies from the Old Testament were fulfilled. When Christ said, " it is finished" it was the time when the Passover lambs were being slain at 3:00 p.m. Making him the rightful Passover Lamb.

If you accept him as the Master of your life, you will be his new bride in the near future, and we will rule and reign on earth with Christ Jesus as kings and priests (Revelation 5:10; 21:2). But until then we must wait for the blessed hope of his return (Titus 2:13). Even though our sins are cleansed, our bodies are still sinful, not yet redeemed. This is why our bodies die but our spirits live on (Romans 8:10). Death physically and spiritually was part of the curse we received in the Garden of Eden and inherited from Adam (Genesis 3:19; Romans 5:12). But Christ's Father was not man but God. Therefore, he was not living in sin. Sin is passed on by our fathers. Because Christ was sinless, he was the only one qualified to take on our sins (2 Corinthians 5:21; Galatians 3:13; 1 Peter 2:22). Christ was unique in a way. No one could take his life. He was born out of sin. Therefore, he would have lived forever. He had to lay his life down willingly for us (John 10:17–18). He was still alive even after the beatings that he received and being nailed to the cross. He outlived and took on more than anyone else could have taken. "He bowed his, head and gave up the ghost," but he still had to give his life up (John 19:30). (We will cover more on the crucifixion shortly.)

The Romans and the priest did carry out his execution. But they could not kill him. They were the means by which his physical punishment was delivered. His whole purpose was to take away our sins. There is nothing that we need to add to what he did in order to receive salvation. The only thing we need to do is to believe in our hearts and confess with our mouths (Romans 10:9). Nowhere does it say, "Behold! Water baptism takes away our sins. Behold! Your works take away your sins. Behold! Your money takes away your sins." No! It says, "Behold the lamb of God that taketh away the sins of the world." This is the only way to eternal life (John 14:6). This is the only payment needed for your salvation, the payment done at Calvary for you!

The Crucifixion

John 19:18–37 says,

> Where they crucified him, and two other with him, on either side one, and Jesus in the midst. And Pilate wrote a title, and put it on the cross. And the writing was JESUS OF NAZARETH THE KING OF THE JEWS. This title then read many of the Jews: for the place where Jesus was crucified was nigh to the city: and it was written in Hebrew, and Greek, and Latin. Then said the chief priests of the Jews to Pilate, Write not, The King of the Jews; but that he said, I am King of the Jews. Pilate answered, What I have written I have written. Then the soldiers, when they had crucified Jesus, took his garments, and made four parts, to every soldier a part; and also his coat: now the coat was without seam, woven from the top throughout. They said therefore among themselves, Let us not rend it, but cast lots for it, whose it shall be: that the scripture might be fulfilled, which

saith, They parted my raiment among them, and for my vesture they did cast lots. These things therefore the soldiers did. Now there stood by the cross of Jesus his mother, and his mother's sister, Mary the wife of Cleophas, and Mary Magdalene. When Jesus therefore saw his mother, and the disciple standing by, whom he loved, he saith unto his mother, Woman, behold thy son! Then saith he to the disciple, Behold thy mother! And from that hour that disciple took her unto his own home. After this, Jesus knowing that all things were now accomplished, that the scripture might be fulfilled, saith, I thirst. Now there was set a vessel full of vinegar: and they filled a spunge with vinegar, and put it upon hyssop, and put it to his mouth. When Jesus therefore had received the vinegar, he said, It is finished: and he bowed his head, and gave up the ghost. The Jews therefore, because it was the preparation, that the bodies should not remain upon the cross on the sabbath day, (for that sabbath day was an high day,) besought Pilate that their legs might be broken, and that they might be taken away. Then came the soldiers, and brake the legs of the first, and of the other, which was crucified with him. But when they came to Jesus, and saw that he was dead already, they brake not his legs: But one of the soldiers with a spear pierced his side, and forthwith came there out blood and water. And he that saw it bare record, and his record is true: and he knoweth that he saith true, that ye might believe. For these things were done, that the scripture should be fulfilled, A bone of him shall not be broken. And again another scripture saith, They shall look on him whom they pierced.

The death of Christ was a very gruesome event. The best way to truly imagine it would be to watch Mel Gibson in *The Passion of the Christ*. He came here to preach the gospel but was rejected by men (Isaiah 53.3). His whole purpose was to take our sins and sorrows to the cross for our redemption.

Isaiah 53:3–12 says,

He is despised and rejected of men; a man of sorrows, and acquainted with grief: and we hid as it were our faces from him; he was despised, and we esteemed him not. Surely he hath borne our griefs, and carried our sorrows: yet we did esteem him stricken, smitten of God, and afflicted. But he was wounded for our transgressions, he was bruised for our iniquities: the chastisement of our peace was upon him; and with his stripes we are healed. All we like sheep have gone astray; we have turned every one to his own way; and the Lord hath laid on him the iniquity of us all. He was oppressed, and he was afflicted, yet he opened not his mouth: he is brought as a lamb to the slaughter, and as a sheep before her shearers is dumb, so he openeth not his mouth. He was taken from prison and from judgment: and who shall declare his generation? For he was cut off out of the land of the living: for the transgression of my people was he stricken. And he made his grave with the wicked, and with the rich in his death; because he had done no violence, neither was any deceit in his mouth. Yet it pleased the Lord to bruise him; he hath put him to grief: when thou shalt make his soul an offering for sin, he shall see his seed, he shall prolong his days, and the pleasure of the Lord shall prosper in his hand. He shall see of the travail of his soul, and shall be satisfied: by his knowledge shall my righteous servant justify many; for he shall bear their iniquities. Therefore will I divide him a portion with the great, and he shall divide the spoil with the strong; because he hath poured out his soul unto death: and he was numbered with the transgressors; and he bare the sin of many, and made intercession for the transgressors.

He was beaten for us under Jewish tradition. He suffered thirty-nine lashes (Isaiah 50:6; 53:5; John 19:1). The Romans were the ones doing the beatings. They did not care what the traditions of Israel were. It could have been more than thirty-nine lashes! This was no ordinary beating. They tore flesh from his body! You would have been able to see his ribs. There was torn flesh dangling from his body. This cruel beating was worse than a severe car accident. Every time they hit him with the whip, it was for us! He went through it just for us. They ripped the hair from his face. It tore the flesh from off of his face (Isaiah 50:6). Can you imagine the pain of having the hair plucked out of your face? I can't even stand to have one hair plucked off of my body! They placed a crown of thrones on his head (Matthew 27:29; John 19:2). All of this was done before he went to the cross! Can you imagine all of the pain our Savior went through? He did that for you and me! Justice had to be served! Someone had to pay the price! Thank God that I do not have to pay that price and that someone paid it for me! God's standards are high, too high for us to meet. So he became flesh, and he met the standards for us. I am so glad that our God is a loving God! He created us, knowing that we would betray him. He came to the earth as flesh only to serve justice on himself that was rightfully ours. That is true love, true romance!

When the soldiers casted lots for his clothing, that fulfilled the prophecies that David had written a thousand years earlier (Psalm 22:18). The soldiers knew that night was approaching. There couldn't be any dead people left out after sunset according to the law (Deuteronomy 21:23). To quicken the death, they broke the legs of the criminals so that they would suffocate. People who were crucified would push themselves up so that they could breathe. When their legs were broken, they could no longer stand to breathe. When they came to Christ, he was already dead not because they had crucified him but because he had given up the Ghost. Instead of breaking his legs, they pierced his side. Blood and water came out, meaning that there was no life left in him. To fulfill Scripture, the Roman soldiers were not to break a bone because Christ was the Passover lamb (Numbers 9:12).

The Resurrection

John 20:11–18 says,

> But Mary stood without at the sepulchre weeping: and as she wept, she stooped down, and looked into the sepulcher, And seeth two angels in white sitting, the one at the head, and the other at the feet, where the body of Jesus had lain. And they say unto her, Woman, why weepest thou? She saith unto them, Because they have taken away my LORD, and I know not where they have

laid him. And when she had thus said, she turned herself back, and saw Jesus standing, and knew not that it was Jesus. Jesus saith unto her, Woman, why weepest thou? whom seekest thou? She, supposing him to be the gardener, saith unto him, Sir, if thou have borne him hence, tell me where thou hast laid him, and I will take him away. Jesus saith unto her, Mary. She turned herself, and saith unto him, Rabboni; which is to say, Master. Jesus saith unto her, Touch me not; for I am not yet ascended to my Father: but go to my brethren, and say unto them, I ascend unto my Father, and your Father; and to my God, and your God. Mary Magdalene came and told the disciples that she had seen the LORD, and that he had spoken these things unto her.

Can you imagine the shock of Mary when she saw our Lord go through the torture for our iniquities and then find his body gone when she went to his tomb? But he wasn't stolen as she had thought. He was resurrected! He defeated death and took the keys of hell (Revelation 1:18).

Satan thought that he defeated Jesus at the grave little did he know was that this is where Christ was about to bruise his head (Genesis 3:14, 15). No other pagan god has ever claimed that defeat. No other god has ever had a life-changing testimony. My God is the only one that has accomplished that. If you are looking for his bones in a tomb, you will not find them! If you want to find out where he is, then you must put your faith in his resurrection, and one day you will find him.

Why would Christ tell her not to touch him? His blood was not yet laid at the altar for the remission of sins (Leviticus 16). He could not allow the sin of Mary's flesh to touch him. It was a commandment for the priest to be perfect for the Day of Atonement. The sins of humanity were paid for, but the sacrifice of sins was not complete until the blood of the Lamb was laid at the altar. Many self-proclaimed gods have come and gone but not my Lord! Buddha, Allah, and other gods may have come, lived, and died, but only one died for you! He went to hell for you and defeated the grave for you! These other gods died, and hell consumed them! *There is power in the resurrection!* If you are planning on making it, then you'd better put your trust in someone who went to hell for you and came out victorious!

What Does It Mean that Christ Came by Water and Blood?

First John 5:6–9 says,

> This is he that came by water and blood,
> even Jesus Christ; not by water only, but
> by water and blood. And it is the Spirit
> that beareth witness, because the Spirit is
> truth. For there are three that bear record in
> heaven, the Father, the Word, and the Holy
> Ghost: and these three are one. And there are
> three that bear witness in earth, the Spirit,
> and the water, and the blood: and these three
> agree in one. If we receive the witness of
> men, the witness of God is greater: for this
> is the witness of God which he hath testified
> of his Son.

Coming by water does not mean that he was born in the water or only God at baptism as some have said.. It is true that there is water present at our birth and that he did come in this world as flesh (John 1:14). Some think that this means he was God between water and blood. If this was the case, then he would not have been resurrected. He is

God, and that is why he defeated death. Death was not the ending of his duty. Nor was water the beginning of his duty. The passage refers to the significance of his baptism. His baptism identifies him as the Son of Man "The sent one by God," as referenced in John 3:16. These are the witnesses. God speaking was a witness. The Holy Spirit descending was a witness. The Son of Man receiving the Holy Spirit during baptism was a witness (Matthew 3:16, 17; Mark 1:10, 11; Luke 3:22; John 1:32). These three witnesses Validated Jesus as the Word made flesh, the Anointed One, the Christ. First John 5: 7 says, that "three bore witness" Just as in the Old and the New Testament two or three were needed to validate the truth (Deuteronomy 19:15; Matthew 18:16).

The baptism was when Christ was anointed with the Holy Spirit to perform the miracles that lay ahead of him (Isaiah 61:1–2; Luke 4:18–19; Acts 10:38). When Christ came by blood, it is reference to the cross, where his blood was shed. All three—the Father, the Son, and the Holy Spirit—agreed on the blood and are one (1 John 5: 8). This makes it very clear that there are three members to the Godhead. Three members of the Godhead was needed to validate the truth in a supernatural way to the natural men who was watching just as it validated it to John the

Baptist (John 1:33). His blood washes you and me clean from sin (Revelation 1:5). Being reconciled to God through the life of Jesus Christ, we received the atonement for sins.

What Must We Do to Have Fellowship with Christ?

First John 1:5–9 (ESV) says,

> This is the message we have heard from him and proclaim to you, that God is light, and in him is no darkness at all. If we say we have fellowship with him while we walk in darkness, we lie and do not practice the truth. But if we walk in the light, as he is in the light, we have fellowship with one another, and the blood of Jesus his Son cleanses us from all sin. If we say we have no sin, we deceive ourselves, and the truth is not in us. If we confess our sins, he is faithful and just to forgive us our sins and to cleanse us from all unrighteousness."

God is a perfect God. We cannot have fellowship with him in heaven unless we are born again. His presence is so glorious that just being near him would consume you as a fire (Hebrews 12:29). Not only that, but you cannot have fellowship with him in this life unless you are in a covenant with him through Jesus Christ (John 9:31).

So many people think they are saved and going to heaven, but they do not bear the fruits of a child of God (Matthew 7:20). Works do not save us, but works are evidence of salvation. We cannot live in darkness and have fellowship with him at the same time. It is either one or the other. If you are saved and know it but are backsliding, you have a barrier of sins blocking you from having a fellowship from him. As a result, you will not be blessed in this life (Deuteronomy 28:15–68). To say that you are a Christian but to act like a sinner is dangerous! Not only is it dangerous, but it is a straight-up lie! You must clean up the sin to restore a fellowship with him.

Christ has taken on our sins for us because we are all sinners. We have all stolen, cheated, hated, and cursed. In some way you have broken his commandment. If you will confess your sins and follow his Holy Spirit, you will be lead into the light to blossom the way Christ wants you to (John 16:13). He will no longer remember your sins (Hebrews 8:12). He will cast your sins into the ocean (Micah 7:19). They will be out of his sight and memory. Our God can choose what he wants to remember about us. He chooses not to remember our sins, but we must ask him to forget about them.

You Are Bought with a Price!

"What? Know ye not that your body is the temple of the Holy Ghost which is in you, which ye have of God, and ye are not your own? For ye are bought with a price: therefore glorify God in your body, and in your spirit, which are God's" (1 Corinthians 6:19–20).

The same passage from the Amplified Bible says, "Do you not know that your body is the temple (the very sanctuary) of the Holy Spirit who lives within you, whom you have received [as a Gift] from God? You are not your own, you were bought with a price [purchased with a preciousness and paid for, made His own]. So then, honor God and bring glory to Him in your body."

Our very own bodies are the temples of God, and the Holy Ghost lives in us. Isn't that amazing? The Holy Spirit lives in us, guiding us, directing us, and comforting us (John 14:17, 26; John 16:13). Once we are born again, we do not belong to ourselves anymore but to the Lord God Almighty. He purchased us with his own blood. As mentioned earlier if you have received the Holy Spirit then you are saved! You do not have to be baptized to receive the Holy Spirit just as the first century saints that I previously listed were not. If you have received the Spirit (Gods free gift) then you are clean; because God does not dwell in an unclean temple.

How many times have we worked hard for something that we truly desire? We dream about it, think about it, and sometimes obsess about it. Christ is the same way with us. He paid the ultimate price for us with his own body and his own soul so that we may become his very own. Now we are his children, and soon we will be his very own brides.

Once we are born again as his children, we need to live with love and show everyone that we are bought with his blood and are saved from dead works by serving a living God (Hebrews 9:14).That is how we live to witness that we are new creatures bought with a price (2 Corinthians 5:17; Galatians 6:15). The price of salvation was so expensive that no one could pay for but God himself. He pays for it and gives it to us as a free gift. One day I was thanking the Lord for giving me a beautiful family, providing me with a job, and most importantly, paying the penalty for my sins. At that moment he said, "You are welcome." Isn't that amazing? That's what a gift is. It is free!

His Blood Gives Us Access to the Throne!

Hebrews 9:11–15 says,

> But Christ being come an high priest of good things to come, by a greater and more perfect tabernacle, not made with hands, that is to say, not of this building; neither by the blood of goats and calves, but by his own blood he entered in once into the holy place, having obtained eternal redemption for us. For if the blood of bulls and of goats, and the ashes of an heifer sprinkling the unclean, sanctifieth to the purifying of the flesh: how much more shall the blood of Christ, who through the eternal Spirit offered himself without spot to God, purge your conscience from dead works to serve the living God? And for this cause he is the mediator of the New Testament that by means of death, for the redemption of the transgressions that were under the first testament, they which are called might receive the promise of eternal inheritance.

A high priest was a supreme leader of the Israelites. The position of the high priest was a hereditary position. It can be traced back all the way to Aaron the brother of Moses (Exodus 28:1). The high priest had to be holy. His daughters had to be virgins (Leviticus 21:1–15). The high priest was above the other priests. The high priest was the mediator between God and man. His responsibility was to represent man. The high priest had to offer an offering of sin once a year for the sins of the whole congregation and for himself.

The high priest's main role was to offer a sacrifice on the Day of Atonement, which came once a year. The high priest was the only one allowed to enter the most holy place behind the veil and stand before God. He brought the blood of the sacrifice into the Holy of Holies and sprinkle it on the mercy seat (Leviticus 16:14, 15) Now Christ has taken his blood into the Holy of Holies, and Jesus became our High Priest. This means that we are all a royal priesthood (1 Peters 2:9). That is every believer man, woman, and child are considered priest with only on mediator between us and God that mediator is Jesus Christ (1 Timothy 2:5). No longer do we need a priest to pray on our behalf. We can pray all by ourselves and turn straight to the throne room of God.

This is accomplished not by the blood of goats and animals but by the blood of God himself at his death. This blood ushered in our New Testament, and we now have the promise of eternal life.

Hebrews 4:14–16 says,

> Seeing then that we have a great high priest, that is passed into the heavens, Jesus the Son of God, let us hold fast our profession. For we have not an high priest which cannot be touched with the feeling of our infirmities; but was in all points tempted like as we are, yet without sin. Let us therefore come boldly unto the throne of grace, that we may obtain mercy, and find grace to help in time of need.

Christ, our high priest, is now in heaven, sitting at the right hand of the Father, making intercession for us (Romans 8:34; Colossians 3:1). No matter how weak at times we may be, no matter how many times we miss it, no matter what our weaknesses are, our sins cannot touch him. He has the right to claim the title of the High Priest for humanity because he stripped himself of no reputation and took upon the form of a servant and was tempted just like you and me but never gave into sin. Can you imagine that? He was tempted with lust, anger, hate, and pride (Hebrews 4:15).

We can now ask the Father in Jesus' name for the things that we need. Whether we need financial assistance to pay a power bill and we do not know what to do next, we can ask for help. We can even ask for the forgiveness of our sins. He is faithful to deliver to us so that our joy may be full (John 16:24). No more sacrifices are needed for the forgiveness of our sins. Forgiveness of sins comes by asking God to wash us clean with the Blood of Christ.

His Blood Gives Us Healing!

Because of the price Jesus paid at Calvary, we can have healing. Isaiah 53:5 says, "By his stripes we are healed." His stripes give us the power to lay hands on the sick and expect them to recover (Mark 16:18; James 5:14–16). Healing was placed on the cross for us. When we call on his name for healing and believe that he has taken care of it, then we will be healed! The cross covered many things for us, not only salvation but his healing power too!

Because of His Blood, We Receive Power!

Because of the sacrifice he made, now we receive his Holy Spirit (Acts 1:8). He guides us in difficult situations and comforts us (John 14:26; 16:13) if we will just listen. This power allows us to proclaim ourselves with boldness as witnesses in the world of Jesus Christ (Mark 16:15; Acts 4:29; Ephesians 6:19). This power is given to all believers (Mark 16:17), not just to preachers but to those who believe. When we have received this power with faith, signs and wonders will follow us to perform miracles (Mark 16:17; Acts 2:43; 4:30; 5:12; 6:8; 15:12; 2 Corinthians 12:12; Hebrews 2:4). These miracles include casting out demons, speaking in tongues, raising the dead, and healing the sick with other various miracles just with the use of his name.

Because of His Blood, We Are Now Considered His Children!

Because of his blood, we are now Christ brothers and sisters, sons of the living God (Matthew 12:50; Romans 8:14). We will sit with Christ in his throne (Ephesians 2:6). We will judge nations and angels (1 Corinthians 6:3). In the New Jerusalem we will rule and reign as kings and priests with Christ Jesus (1 Peter 2:9; Revelation 1:6; 5:10; 20:6). All of this we will inherit as sons and daughters of the almighty God. That is the heritage of our Lord, paid for it by the blood of the Lamb.

Because of His Blood, We Have Eternal Life!

Eternal life is a gift from God so that we may have fellowship with him (Romans 6: 23). The gift from God is his Son, Jesus Christ (John 3:16). The Son of God made a way for us to gain eternal life by the sacrifice of his own body and the pouring out of his own blood. All we must do to receive this free gift of eternal life is to believe in the name of the Son of God. Then we will have eternal life (1 John 5:13).

Conclusion

Now at the conclusion of *Why My Blood Is Enough*, I hope you now have a better understanding of what Christ has done for us and you know that his blood is enough, that salvation is not achieved through baptism, but that baptism is a command we should obey. Works do not earn salvation. Works are necessary to promote the kingdom, and it shows the fruit of the Spirit to others that Christ is our Savior. The law does not save you; however, it is good because it points out sin in your life if you are not following the Spirit, and it shows sinners that they need Christ because they have broken God's standards. If you need a new life and new beginning because you cannot do it on your own and you feel uncertain of your fate, you can rely on his blood as payment for the sins that you have committed. His blood is what you can count on. If you feel like you are uncertain about your eternal destination, you should say a prayer right now.

You can pray, "God I know that you sent your only Son to die in my place for me on the cross and resurrected three days later from the grave. I ask that you will forgive me of my sins. I believe in my heart and confess with my mouth that Jesus Christ is my Lord and Savior. In your Son's name, I pray. Amen."

When you prayed that prayer, all of heaven rejoiced at that moment with you. That was the most important thing in your life you could have ever done! Now you are called to be a witness to others and tell them what Christ has done for us. May God bless you!